MOMENT to MOMENT

Notes to Self

SAVITA SAHNI

PARTRIDGE

To order additional copies of this book, contact
Partridge India
000 800 10062 62
orders.india@partridgepublishing.com

www.partridgepublishing.com/india

Dedicated to my parents -in- law:

Late Vidyavati Sahni.
Late Satya Dev Sahni

And my parents,

Late Shakuntala Saini (AIR,TV Veteran Drama Artist)
Late Jai Dayal Saini.

Acknowledgements

I would like to thank my husband, Arvind Bhushan Sahni who has always believed in me and supported me in my efforts to write.

I also owe my thanks to my loving siblings and friends who enjoyed reading 'The Bottom Line' my first book and motivated me to continue writing. Finally, I am grateful to The Partridge Publishing Team for turning my dream book into reality.

1

Give yourself a break.
You are the master of your fate.
You have to collect pearls of wisdom.
They are not found in any kingdom.
Peel off the veils from your face,
Real life is the stage.
Get into the groove,
Master all the moves.
Strenuous as it is,
Don't let it tire you,
It is only devotion to your work,
That makes you overcome the rough and tough.

2

Don't ever chase anybody
If you want to get them.
Make yourself attractive enough,
Let them find out the real you.
You are absolutely lovable.
Your adorable ways are winsome.
Your willingness to be there for others,
Whenever they need you,
Leaves no doubt that you are caring,
You are concerned,
You never let anybody down.
Your qualities will attract others.
So take it easy.
Let them discover you.
Don't lose patience.
They will.
If they don't,
They don't deserve you!

3

I know you from inside out.

When you give the hint of a smile

I know what's going on in your mind.

When you shout at somebody,

I know the reason why.

When you are upset,

I know how to bring you back.

Your moods change fast.

Now irritated,now calm.

Now cheerful, now moody.

When angry you are almost crazy.

You are cheerful when you like your food,

God save you if it isn't that good!

Your expressions are a mystery,

But soon I discover their history.

You go wild if rubbed the wrong way.

But within seconds your mood sways.

You are back to your sweet ways.

You have to accept people as they are.

They have no control over what they are.

They have been made in a certain mould.

They are what they are by default,all told.

It is their genes which design their traits & faults.

Your love for them should be unconditional,

They may not express their love but its real.

Nobody is black or white.
Give them a break,
They will do what it takes.
They will win your heart,
Just give them a chance.

4

When did I have my first crush?
Perhaps when I was all of fourteen!
Just an eye contact with a guy,
Sent me flying to a different sky.
Every handsome man was potentially a mate.
But I had to concentrate on examination dates
Priorities,man, priorities !
If I remained illiterate and unemployed,
Nobody decent would offer to make me his bride..
Gloating over books to mug up the highlights,
Pictures of heroes swum before my eyes.
Still managed to be promoted to the next class,
By hook or by crook I managed to pass.
Completed post graduation,
And landed a job at last.
Had great time teaching college kids,
Love did happen at a crucial point.
But a dutiful daughter that I was.
I ignored the reverberations of infatuation.
And chose to marry someone already chosen.
It was a disaster from the start.
All my dreams fell apart.
An Indian girl is a sacrificial goat.
She is offered to a family,
As a gift with great pomp & show.

She is assumed to be living happily,
Even though between the couple,
There is no compatibility,
After all she breaks bread with them
Gives them children and respectability.
This perception turns full circle,
When her children, in turn,get married.
The cycle goes on,
Without any discussion on,
What constitutes a happy marriage.

5

If you wish to ignore somebody,
You pretend to be busy.
Why can't you be frank?
Why can't you yell back?
Nobody tells you not to.
Being diplomatic is practical.
But you can discard toxic people.
After all, You have to survive.
Keeping wrong company is not nice.
Have faith in your convictions.
Go ahead with confidence.
Never be that diffident.
Being bold and beautiful,
Being fast and furious,
Being smart and serious,
Being friendly and gregarious,
Being trendy and fashionable,
Will help you become your own person.
You will not be just another person.
You will impress intellectual fraternity,
You will lead a life of quality.
You might even grow into a celebrity.
It is not an unrealistic plan.
Everything is possible for man.
All your energy must be tapped,

So that you can continue to tread,

A peaceful path,earn your bread.

Everybody hankers after peace,

You climb mountains you can't reach.

Suffering chastens you,

You pass endurance test.

And stay at your best.

You shouldn't get intimidated by anyone.

Be bold and learn to face everyone.

6

Your hand written notes on literature,
Still can be found among things I treasure.
You got entry into my home,
On the pretext of sharing notes.
We chatted over a cup of tea.
We discussed T S Eliot or Keats.
But your eyes wandered beyond,
You noticed only what I had put on.
Gave me compliments in an undertone.
You often came to see me.
And tried your best to impress me.
Yet nothing made a dent anywhere.
I found a good friend in you.
I tried but didn't feel a thing for you.
I had definitely had no crush on you.
Sometimes you mistake liking for love.
You are fooled into believing you love.
You learn your lessons a little too late.
Much time is wasted over such class mates,
Perhaps this way you know their intent.
Give them up and gradually move on
In due time you find your true icon.

7

Fame is so nebulous,
It isn't for every one of us.
You strive to get it.
You are visible at shows.
Create a presence of sorts.
Write something truly witty,
Keeping in mind the nitty gritty.
Express ideas galore
Narrate ancient folklore.
Cry your heart out,
To demolish crooks.
Scribble a cook book,
While nibbling something,
By the side of a brook.
Achieve the top most slot,
As a shrewd politician.
Become a statesman,
Not a magician.
Be the head of a multinational.
Let your business go international..
Earn medals as an athlete.
Get decorated for badminton or tennis.
Vie for National Awards.
In any category including war.
Create history,

Break records.
Save precious lives,
When disaster strikes
People who continue to excel,
Carve a name for themselves.
But doing anything worthwhile,
Demands perseverance, tenacity.
Vision and the risk taking capacity.
Without effort you can't even catch a train.
Creativity demands the use of your brain.
You don't really go after fame,
It comes automatically to you.
If you rise and make your name.

8

Earth doesn't indulge in self healing,
Pollution with its soot is killing.
Rains do oblige once in a while.
The city CM tries to keep it green.
But the traffic is mean.
Nature has a dual face.
It cheers you but it harms you too.
Floods, earthquakes,lightening,
Tsunami destroy you.
The sky looks longingly at the Earth.
But the curtain of smoke hides its girth.
Man is an intelligent animal.
He should realise it is terrible
To let Earth turn Hitler.
Think of something fast.
Take action,be smart
Employ tactics to outsmart,
The genie which has put to ransom our hearts.

9

You can't force somebody to read.
If the cover of a book is attractive,
You move towards it.
Hold it in your hands.
Shuffle the pages,
Get caught in a dialogue.
You like it.
Turn a few more pages.
Shift closer to a wall.
Rest against it.
Keep reading engrossed.
Forget everything else.
You come out of this reverie,
When you are told to buy it.
Your mind is already made up.
You pay up, collect the book,
Leave the shop with a smile on your face.
Your day is made.

10

Time is difficult to manage,
You can eat, pray or love,
Still there is time enough.
You can invite friends home,
Go shopping off and on.
Cook, dust,shift things here and there,
Stich buttons or polish silver ware,
Go to social media sites,
Check your likes as you sit or lie.
Restlessness is difficult to keep at bay,
If not busy try to make hay while the cat is away.
What does that mean anyway?
Let there be Sun shine,
When the rats play.
Mr. Bumble bee, Mr. Restless guy,
Don't rack your brain,
There is plenty one can do.
Call a friend on your mobile.
Time will run several miles.
Chatting too is time consuming,
It may,though, be just time killing,
But it diverts your mind,
Fills the emptiness of your life.
You can chat on and on,
Discuss a million things along.

Never let depression catch you,
Just find something to do.
Why not think of doing things by hand.
Get into creative writing or join a band.
If you gauge the depths of your mind,
There will be treasure enough to fill your life.
Let not emptiness plague your life.
If you are young enough,
Take up a job that you like.
If old sleep a while.
Feel fresh and feel fine.

I wait,wait and wait,
Standing forlorn at the gate.
My eyes soaked with tears,
With a look that shows fear.
You are due today from the front,
I am not sure if you would come.
But hoping against hope,
I extend my hand to touch you.
Sense your presence at home.
Your footsteps can be heard.
There is a flutter of birds.
My ears perk up,
I eagerly look up.
Rush towards the door,
Creating impact on the floor.
The door opens wide,
It is dark outside.
The figure with a suitcase.
Approaches the gate.
I reach out to him,
But doubt if it's him.
To dispel darkness,
He flicks open a lighter.
I can see better.
The glitter in my eyes,

Brightens my smiles.
It is him no doubt.
Tears of joy flow copiously,
Giving no space emotionally,
To say much immediately.
We hug each other tightly.
Nothing else matters really.
It is a tough life for men in forces.
Yet they are the most patriotic of the lot,
They are called at any time for any slot.
Ever ready to fight for the nation,
We salute them for their devotion.
Their family comes second.
They would like to spend time with them.
But their loyalty to the nation overrides everything else.

12

What is Fake Book all about?
All your personal information is out.
What you like or what you share,
Your comments,your photos rare,
It is an obsession beyond doubt.
You are added to clubs without your consent.
You may be offended by the content.
They are titled Naughty After Forty,
Exclusive Adult themes or Dead Poets' Society.
You connect to pictures of friends & family.
Sometimes you feel you have slept for ages.
As friends from donkey's years ago,
Say, 'What's up? 'As if you had last seen them
A day before.
Fake Book, no doubt, is addictive..
Every time you look at your mobile,
You are tempted to find out the' likes'.
You frown if you find none.
You roll down the screen quite often,
To find some inspiring quotations,
Some awesome photo shoots,
Long lost friends or interesting news.
Your vanity dictates what to post.
You can't afford to look like a ghost.
People you may not have heard of,

Want to be friends to add to the score.
Friends were never so easy to make.
Just a touch of your finger intentionally,
Or by mistake,
You don't meet over a cup of coffee.
You don't need any Burger or Sushi.
Cheerfully you keep pressing 'like',
Pleasing friends and strangers alike.
You don't have to say," Lets go Dutch."
No cash is required but you must trust.
You begin to recall nostalgic memories.
Post or repost heart wrenching stories.
You have a platform to showcase your art,
Photography, paintings, music or DIY arts.
You accidently or incidentally learn a lot.
All said and done,it is too much of a distraction.
I would rather read a book or cook Mexican,
I have strong likes & dislikes.
I don't share my things so easily.
Why then expend your energy,
On new-fangled social sites for friendship.
Hello,my little circle of close friends,
Lets catch up a movie on week ends.
Coffee or tea is fine to relate to friends.
Instead of impromptu likes, or comments.
Fake Book is a side kick, following the trends.
Those who hate travelling.
Those who like invitations to Candy Crush,

Criminal Cases on the go,
Those who are into multitasking,
Chatting or Advertising.
Who want company all the time,
Who take breaks from work,
To say 'hi' and 'hello' to friends in bulk.
Who are completely in love with themselves.
May be seeking brides or grooms for themselves.
Who change their profile picture as quickly,
As they change their mind.,
Have found a blessing in their Fake Book time line.
Thumbs up for those who use it.
Most log on to it when they wish to smile.

13

A smile
A hand shake,
A hello !
A hi !
A hug.
What's up?
How's life?
What's going on?
Long time no see!
All greetings connect you to friends.
On line or real life.
Being warm in your expressions,
Makes others your instant friends.
If your approach is clinical,
Your words are mechanical,
You come across as a dry person.
You lack warmth in your intention.
You may convey your thoughts,
But your feelings don't go across.
Do learn the art of being polite
It adds another dimension to your life

14

My soul and my body live together like friends,
One can't live without the other.
But strangely my soul stays on the back burner,
Never needing attention or asserting itself.
I constantly worry about my health.
My heart, my stomach, my kidneys,my liver.
I am aware of my soul only when I pray.
Ironically even then I pray to keep me disease free.
Is my soul peaceful?
It never complains
It stays calm & balanced.
As if teaching my body a lesson.
It is the guardian of my sanity.
It is the keeper of my conscience.
I guess when I suffer due to any ABC reason,
It is there to hold me steady.
It shows my strength in times of adversity.
It pushes me to smile.
It sometimes makes me cry.
When I show concern and worry about others,
It is definitely my soul which rises to the occasion,
To take action to help others.
My soul,you are not tangible,
But without you I am a nobody.
I would die without you,

Please guide me how to pray.

I am alive so I exist and speak my mind.

My body and me are intriguingly one.

Without one another we can't exist.

God, teach me to nourish my soul.

I am my soul.

My body is its home.

I worry more about the body,

As it needs to stay healthy.

A perfect soul stays in a perfect body.

15

What remains a mystery,
Strangely attracts you.
Your curiosity grips you.
It gets the better of you.
You wait for the story to unfold.
You turn page after page,
Wanting to know the tale.
As it unfolds you are glued to it,
Forgetting to eat or drink.
Suspense is killing.
You are dying to know,
Who is the jewel thief?
Who is the serial killer?
Who kidnapped the kids?
Who really loved the queen?
Who died tragically?
Who lived to tell the tale?
What moral the story gives?
It is edge of the seat thriller.
You won't budge,
Until you find the killer.
Apart from such fiction,
You read page turners,
Of Biographies, Poetry
Religious or motivational,

Literature.
Watch Ted, Flipboard,
You Tube or Chat shows,
Sermons or musical performances,
Of budding talents, rising stars,
On the horizon of drama or films.
With so much going on,
If you have time,
Life will remain fine.
Reading is a solo pleasure,
But social networking sites connect you to,
Big shots even small fry in great measure.
Stay interested and enjoy,
Books, music, chats, drama,
The entire treasure!

16

Save the girl child,
The topic is not mild.
It is born out of an act of crime.
It takes place in rural background.
A female foetus in a womb is not allowed.
It is aborted when detected in ultrasound.
The cry of the girl child is never heard.
She is strangled before her birth.
What have I done?
She agonisingly asks.
Why do you think I have no heart?
Why can't I see the beauty of this world?
Why can't I smile and love?
Why can't you give me a chance to step out of the womb?
Why am I in a tomb instead of a womb?
I am not allowed to bloom?
I look after all of you men.
If I am decimated,
The world will be annihilated.
Who will bear your progeny?
Who will you marry?
There won't be too many to wed.
Men will go to other countries to wed,
When the sex ratio is skewed.
You can't afford to stay mute.

Speak up O gutsy, educated men.

Save the girl child, save women.

She guards you all along your life.

She nourishes you,

She brings you up right.

So that you grow strong,healthy & wise.

Let her also be born,

Grow up & be strong.

She marches shoulder to shoulder with men.

Excels in fields which so far were confined to men.

She can be spotted in every profession.

Why must you destroy her life before her birth?

You will realise her worth,

When there are not enough women in the world.

It would be a dry, flat, colourless,empty and dull world.

Men will yearn for a woman's love,

Nothing would compare with her.

Wake up O men,

Halt this foeticide,

Let the girl child too grow your alongside.

17

You were born once upon a time.

You owe your life to a couple sublime.

The world calls them parents.

But you must not hang on to them.

Your umbilical cord was severed.

You were now your own person.

Mother's milk was needed for a time.

She gave it to you without a dime.

She was a medium to land you on earth.

She gave up her youth to bring you up.

Father worked to give you sustenance.

He tried his best to give you education.

If you just sit back and go to social networking sites.

You are party to a crime.

You are just amusing yourself

But displeasing your parents.

You are just killing time.

Go hunt for a suitable job.

Earn to support your old parents,

Your young wife and children.

You are a burden on society,

You are a disgrace to your family.

Such cases of young unemployed men,

Are plenty in our society now and then.

Either they have no inclination to work.

Or they don't find suitable work.

Either way they are a pitiable sight.

If they don't mind or even if they mind.

How can they even think of sitting idle,

Feeding on the bounty of their idols?

The worst sights you see in life,

Are those of men whiling away their time,

Not working in their prime.

I pray to you young men.

Your family wishes you to shine.

Stop being a bully, a useless fellow.

Develop self confidence.

Dive into the world.

Try your luck.

If you work towards a goal.

You will find a suitable role.

Your family will flourish

You will get compliments,

You will find a foothold,

In the social rung.

You will once in a while,

Greet your FB or What's App

Friends on your Time Line.

18

A good ball bounces back.
A boomerang is meant to come back.
Do we ever notice what comes back,
What is held back?
If you are courteous with others,
They too will treat you with courtesy.
If you are rude you get a rude reply.
Though there are some who don't reply in kind,
They are so evolved they are perennially nice.
'Tit for tat' was invented by a practical man.
So was 'an eye for an eye'.
But peaceful people don't harbour revenge,
They try to patch up with the vilest of men.
Such men sure are saintly,
They survive on being good mostly.
Law of averages, however, states,
'What goes around comes around'
So try not to get into brawls.
Don't throw stones at others.
Don't hit or abuse.
Stay honest & true
The less you get into rows,
The more you will get wows.

19

Life is strange at times.
Two people die at the same time.
The one dies after having been at the top.
The other one is hanged to death on the dot.
Destiny ordains every man's role on Earth.
But God gives an opportunity to every one.
To renew themselves with their actions.
They can rebuild life slowly without tension.
God sits amused like a judge,
Watches everything that is done.
Giving a free hand to man,
To improve his condition as he can.
Of course the strings are in his hands.
As he plays with them time and again.
He basically designs birth and death.
Man has no control over them.
Birth control methods not withstanding.
Research is done manifold over death of many.
But man gives in to God's insidious plans.
He has over and over again tried to pan,
The systems of birth and death which ran.
He accepts God's supremacy over the world.
Bows to him in the Church, Masjid or Temple.
He fails to understand the criminal community,
Murders, rapes, terror attacks & insanity.

Yet admits there are honest, clean souls,
Who change their life style and much more.
Stay healthy, happy,knowledgeable and bold.
God is as much with us as our breath.
He gives a long rope to man to avoid death.
The wise ones follow his diktats.
The foolish ones keep their ego intact.
Jump the queue to get rich quick.
In the bargain lose themselves by treat or trick.
God smugly smiles at their foolishness.
Takes them away with lawful impediments.
He rewards the industrious and honest souls.
They thus rise,get recognition with medals galore.
Life is not exactly X=Y
Life is never mathematically right.
Just pray to God to improve your life.

20

Plato's Republic is just a drill.
I have yet to see men who fit the bill.
Some may try to build up their body
But they are not intellectually ready
You try to explore the best specimen,
From USA, Australia, India and London.
But getting them together is not exactly fun.
If you shortlist a group which meets the standard
To be trained to rule the world and prosper.
You are unsure if Plato will approve your plan.
His vision and your mission might clash.
The modern world runs on dead lines.
They suffice to sustain their life style.
Brain storming and interchange of ideas,
Gives birth to intelligent conclusions.
All hypotheses culminate in suggestions.
Ideas are implemented,tested for performance.
If they lead to progress in every area decided,
Assuming that all disciplines are interconnected.,
Life runs smoothly without thoughts of worry.
Dear Plato,nobody wants to be exactly like you.

So stay in your book safe and sound.

Nobody wants you to be around.

Agree or disagree with our routine.

The world loves everything to live.

21

I have grown at a certain speed.
Childhood Influences shaped me.
So did the lessons in youth.
Worked at my protruded contours,
Much as a sculptor chisels,
I was given special takes and retakes
I developed my attitude.
My preferences and life style.
Facing myself as I was, was tough.
I didn't have what I found in others.
I realised to my chagrine,I wasn't the best.
Learning comes by and by after a hard test.
It is a continuous process, a life long thing.
You have some talent which is quite unique.
Work at your self, your special edge,
You will use it as a tool to climb the hedge.
Failure is often a guest unwanted, though.
But you take it as a stepping stone
That's the only way to rise in life.
Just keep going riding the tumultuous tide.

Getting everything you want in life is tough.
But having a sense of balance is enough
You will have a reasonably good life.
Earn enough to live in style.

22

Those days were so innocuous.
Vendors kept taking rounds of the square.
Selling veggies,tempting chaats and ice cream,
Shawls, carpets, steel utensils and designer Jeans.
Every time you heard some noise,
You rushed to see what you could try.
Life was so colourful and carefree,
You thought of only home work,exams and what to eat.
You looked forward to the evening to go out and play,
Friends were overjoyed to see you join in some game.
You wore smart sports gear with canvas shoes,
Had a Bata rubber ball which bounced back to you.
Father fixed a net in the space in front of your house.
You could play badminton, volleyball or just run around.
Boys and girls played together without any hassles.
They felt perfectly at ease with each other.
Running a race and cycling was very popular,
So was playing with hula hoop and marbles.
Childhood was all about activities of all sorts.
School was important but lots of fun, of course.
Competition wasn't heard of in academics.
You went to the next class with comfort and ease.
As you grew older your activities increased.
You looked often into the mirror
Selfies were not in fashion then.

But you tried your best to look better.

Who were you trying to impress?

Perhaps you were vying with your friends.

I guess you just felt more confident

If you dressed well.

You got more compliments than them.

I think crushes happen,

When you cross your teens

Every suave guy attracts your attention.

One who gives you admiring looks

Finally wins you over.

Alas! Final is seldom final.

After struggling with yourself,

Alternating between studies and emotions,

Your common sense prevails.

Every body in your life is derailed.

Your text books, your tutorials hook you all the time,

Your special friends have to face the betrayal.

After being decorated with degrees,

You become finally examinations free.

What relief, what sense of pride !

It sends you a few notches high.

Childhood was over years ago.

Youth was quite frustrating,

As you had multiple options to choose from.

Either you got married or got a job.

What job and which man?

Such thoughts distracted you,

Again and again.
Life goes on never giving you a minute to relax.
There are always issues you must understand.
Life passes by giving you ample opportunities,
To enrich everyday of your life span.

23

I have been cooking all my life.

As a daughter, a roommate or a wife.

What to cook is the eternal problem?

If you are with friends you show off a bit,

Chinese fried rice,Mexican tacos are a hit.

Banana cake, quiche,pies or dumpukht.

Diet Catch, coconut water or orange juice

Are the essentials in the party menu.

Ice-cream,fruit cream, or custard pudding

Are the deserts to everybody's liking.

If you are married to a guy who loves food.

You cook day and night to prove,

That you are a good wife cum cook.

But try as hard as you might,

The food is never cooked right.

There is less salt, more sugar,

Vegetable is not cut to the right size,

He goes on making a list of faults he finds.

His mother was the best cook in the world.

A mere wife,young or old, is never an expert.

If perchance he happens to like something.

He wants you to serve that often not just anything.

Your marriage is at risk,

if at lunch or dinner time,

Your friends take you out to dine.

If you want to save your marriage,
Always keep the kitchen fire going.
It is food, food, food and food,
That keeps him in a good mood.

24

After years of slavery
A country gets freedom.
That is taken as a first step,
To your progress in all respect.
Your journey begins with your own government.
You elect them to your best intent.
Expecting to get your respect restored.
In your own eyes and the world.
Your leaders who fought for your rights.
Are treated as honest,hard working and upright.
The poorest citizen supports them.
Hoping to work miracles for themselves.
What is at stake are basic human needs,
A roof over your head, food to survive
Sufficient funds that work provides.
A place to live, medical care, potable water,
Healthy environment, good roads matter.
Our freedom fighters struggled to give us this gift.
Went to jails, suffering inhuman treatment but didn't give in.
They shouted slogans to show their patriotic fervour.
Some brave hearts who defied the rulers had to face
Torture.
But they refused to submit,
They gave up their life for their country.
We,the people should remember them,

When work is halted in the Rajya Sabha,
It is as good as obstructing progress,
It is denying the countrymen their largesse.
A peaceful debate goes a long way.
It opens a path to pass important bills with finesse.
Country comes first, everything else later.
Open your minds O misguided members,
Your country has to follow schemes for welfare.
We may have travelled six decades in freedom,
But the poorest of us have yet to get rid of fiefdom.
We depend on loans,rains,seeds and sufficient land.
Suicides,corruption, exploitation,lack of guidance,
Still touch us though by now we should have moved further.
We should have had basic facilities. education and finances.
Freedom must be guarded to run the nation.
We must work towards a happy,healthy, nation.

Woman you are dynamite.

Don't you deny it.

You can bring about a change in society.

Just be a little more forward to lead.

Collect your wits together.

Be aware of your wings and feathers.

If you make up your mind.

You can move and shake the world right.

There is nothing where you can't step in.

Your sheer presence should bring in,

Some awe, order and discipline.

You are first a woman,

Then a daughter,sister,

Wife or mother.

You play each role emotionally.

You justify them fully.

Your strength comes to the fore,

When you step out of the door.

You carve your place for yourself,

In whatever field you choose to select.

Your strength of mind and character,

Prove your mettle.

You shine in all situations that matter.

Forging ahead keeping your head high,

You earn a name for yourself in time.

Your family supports you to stay in the lime light.

The society acknowledges your might.

You register your capabilities,

Your qualities and faculties.

Your EQ and IQ,

You force the men folk to join the queue.

Without you nothing will complete the view.

You reign and occupy the queen's seat.

Your attitude and confidence,

Will inspire respect at once.

Stay strong,decisive and gutsy.

You will never be weak and flimsy.

You will count,

Without doubt.

26

I never knew friends turn into foes.
They will go to any length to satisfy their egos.
The moment they realise they have lagged behind you
By hook or by crook they weave webs to capture you.
If that doesn't work, they tell white lies behind your back.
So that others are misguided and go off the track.
Sometimes they succeed in back stabbing you.
Leaving you livid,frustrated,rattled and bruised.
How must we treat such friends?
Discard them right away or take revenge.
You don't want to degrade yourself by stooping so low.
You must stay dignified,indifferent and go slow.
Events have a way of turning out in your favour,
If you wait and watch,let life take its own course.
It is very strange that people should feel insecure,
Even after being successful and mature.
The urge to outsmart others is strong in them.
I wish they just compete with themselves.
Using others to achieve their ends is mean.
If they want to remain friends they must act clean.
They malign themselves, when they choose falsehood,
To have an upper hand over those who are honest and good.

27

Sometimes you look back,
Relive your past but lose the track.
There were phases you went through,
When you were terribly sick,
When fate was not kind a bit.
Still your mental strength was a weapon.
It took you across free of tension.
Higgledy piggledy life went ahead.
Quality of life was not exactly great.
Shouldering your responsibilities,
Aware of the burden you carried,
Your day today life was harried.
Often you were pensive to see your plight.
But you had no way to divert your mind.
There was no time for entertainment
To have an exercise regime or self improvement.
Where does planning for one's life begin?
Ideally,it should begin before your birth.
You should not just be delivered any day on Earth.
God takes a chance with you.
Parents too take a chance with you.
You are conceived out of boredom or passion.
Whichever way, you come into this world,
Rich or poor,bright or dull,weak or tough.
Even if you are planned, it is still a chance.

You can't exactly pre plan your entrance?
Your parents at this age can't divine your future.
Whatever their means,they just try to nurture.
When everything related to you is uncertain,
We don't expect you to be in anyway certain.
If God plays with your life, everybody does.
All life long you play hide and seek.
Never sure about what happens in between.
This balancing act takes a toll on you.
You grow old faster than God intended you to.
God's plans are unfathomable.
You can't penetrate them ever.
You accept them as your destiny.
You offer prayers but can't pressurise anybody.
That's life for everybody!

28

The vacant seat reminds you,
It had an occupant a minute ago.
The seat is still warm,
Exuding the warmth of his presence.
Is he going to be back?
Perhaps not.
There is nothing here to detain him.
No loved ones.
Nobody who cares.
Nobody who needs him.
He had come for an interview.
Obviously he didn't get the coveted post.
But he did charm me with his good looks,
His sunny small talk.
His desire to make it big in life.
A young bright lad,
With a sense of humour,
His cheerful response to anybody,
Who cared to share his chitchat.
I was just a distant stranger,
Watching him shine.
I didn't react to anything he had said,
But strangely once he got up and disappeared,
I felt a vacuum,
As if after ages I had a peep at an affectionate,

Amiable, tall,dark and handsome hulk,
Who I would have loved to marry.
Had I been young & marriageable !
How utterly ridiculous !
Even at grand ma's age,
I could think of marriage!
Perhaps a woman never grows old.
At heart she is always a young woman.
Signs of age not withstanding.
And whoever she had chosen to marry,
There is always a dream man she cherishes.

29

Life repeats itself.
If you have set habits,
You tend to stick to them.
Your day is structured to include,
Whatever is important to you.
Sometimes you are driven by compulsions,
Which you are obliged to follow.
But on the whole you master your time.
If your will power is strong,
You use your time to your advantage.
More often than not,
Your duties outweigh your demands.
Try as you might you can't hold on to time,
Twist it to fill it with something you like.
There are time or money constraints.
You also don't assert yourself too much.
For fear it might eat into the time you give to family.
If you do manage to squeeze into some time slot,
When you can go out to watch a film or a play,
You can't find suitable transport or company
It is again you who are at fault.
You should have managed your life well.
Everybody must earn,
Everybody must learn to drive.
Everybody must do things they like.

You are as important as your family.

You don't have to relegate yourself to the back burner.

If you don't love yourself,

You can't love anybody else.

Others can only inspire you to do things.

It is you who has to propel yourself to action.

Depression is your enemy.

You begin to sink if you withdraw into yourself.

Meet, interact, organise, participate,

If you wish to stay at the stake.

30

You got your freedom on a platter.
You have read details which matter.
You get goose bumps to hear the tales,
Of your country men who went to jails,
Fighting for independence from the English,
Who perpetrated crimes on your citizens,
Your men non-violently waged the war of freedom.
They were tortured for daring to defy them.
But our brave hearts refused to bend.
They gave up their lives to give you this land.
The struggle they carried on lasted many years.
The atrocities they bore were unimaginable.
They lived a threadbare existence,
Barely managed to run the kitchen on pittance.
But the fire within them was kept alive.
Their true love for the nation
The unity,strength and intention,
Showed in their resolve to get you back your nation.
There is no doubt that you cherish your freedom.
You do elect your own government.
Various parties have come and gone,
But unfortunately your country still lags behind,
In education, standard of living, financial status,
Population control, sanitation, housing and agriculture.
Although a democracy,you still believe in divisive politics.

You don't let the government work to the nation's benefit.
Party is supreme for the opposition alliances.
The country is irresponsibly relegated to the back burner.
Every issue that concerns the safety or progress of the people,
Becomes an agenda for political debates on the media.
Which should actually be healthy,
But it turns into a battle bitter and lengthy.
All the participants are just out to strangle each other.
The real issue gets side tracked, the nation suffers,
Sessions in Parliament go the pandemonium way.
Nothing decisive gets underway.
Reforms in the interest of both masses and elite,
Keep on getting postponed due to indiscipline,
Confusion,disorder, discourtesy and disrespect.
Very few members show restraint and attention,
To the speaker and the ruling party's declarations.
Chaos reigns, no constructive work gets done.
Some misguided leaders provoke innocent villagers,
To shout slogans against the government at rallies,
When it is election time in some states.
They just adamantly, vehemently reject any reforms,
Without any rhyme or reason.
Their agenda is just to malign the current rulers.
Where does the country come in?
It is side tracked to bring them in.
A determined Prime Minister sticks to his guns.
Keeps his ministers on edge to carry on his work.
A large country with a large population,

Can work wonders if there are no personal ambitions,
Country takes precedence over everything else.
With so much potential the nation would take long strides.
If dirty politics is kept at bay or kept aside.
With so much land,natural wealth, young people,
The country can regain its golden past,
Flourish in trade, culture and education fast.
Let good sense, loyalty to nation prevail.
You shall leave an enviously happy trail

31

If I was twenty five again,
What would I change?
Everything about me, I guess.
I would never take up the career,
Which gobbled up all I held dear.
Learning a craft or playing an instrument,
Socialising with relatives or friends,
Going on family trips or functions,
Dress up in the evening to look fresh,
To charm my husband and meet neighbours,
To dine out in style not just walk a mile.
To follow an exercise regime or diet,
To learn skills of driving, stitching or painting
To get into reading, creative writing or tatting.
To do short term courses on baking or cooking.
Well, well!
A whole life has passed by.
My work disabled everything I wanted to try,
To work on me or improve my life style.
Oh to be young again!
With all that learning or training,
I would have made better choices in life.
More confident, more sure you are.
Quality of life gets better by far.
You understand more,

You achieve more.

Time occupies both work and pleasure.

Keeps you gainfully busy and have leisure.

My young friends take a lesson from me.

There should be 'me time' or 'time free'.

To pamper yourself and the family.

32

What if each one had to do something,
To make life easy.
They would first make a vehicle which,
Lifted up by itself if stuck in traffic.
They would make robots to work for you.
Getting the work done to suit you.
They would create disposable clothes.
You will have countless designer dresses in store.
Everybody would try to have essential things.
Only must haves will occupy the space within.
Shopping would be done only on line.
You will be delivered the product,
Within no time.
Like the multiple knife one exercise device,
Will contain options to keep you fit and fine.
You didn't have to always formulate
Your thoughts in words.
Brains will communicate with each other,
Emotions will stay subdued.
You will never lose your cool.
You would nonchalantly do whatever you
Liked.
Provided it wasn't illegal or unkind.
Every search engine will have voice commands,
It will give you ideas to make a million yarns.

Everything invented will make life easier.

Life will be fun all round the year.

There wouldn't be any crime.

Nobody would commit suicide.

Nobody would be terminally sick.

The world would be easier to live in.

Every problem would be put in a bin.

Politics would be fair and clean.

You would get votes if you had solid

Reforms in your agenda,

You would be voted out mid term if you

Didn't fulfil your fundas,

Barring impractical things life could,

Certainly be made fair and straight.

Let us not complain.

Instead invent things.

Think, think and think again.

Pick up educational and motivational links.

They would provide you inspiration to win.

Technology would be a permanent fixture.

Life's quality will be surely much better.

33

I wish some times that I was a man.

They look so tough with muscles so fat.

Their hair is usually short,

They don't have to make plaits or knots.

They have hair all over their body,

But they don't wax their legs, arms or upper lip.

They flaunt their chest whenever or where ever they want.

They don't have to face any taunts.

Grand mothers and mothers spoil them no end.

Everything in the kitchen is made at their request.

Mothers,sisters,daughters or spouses,

All allow them to throw their weight around.

Their word is final whatever might the other members feel.

Women have to bow down and grind their teeth.

Decisions are often made collectively.

But the last word is that of the head of the family.

A man walks with long strides,

Modesty is not an issue to keep in mind.

Women stick to domestic topics when they chat,

The men choose current political scenario,

Fiscal health of the nation, Sensex or vat.

They are big drama kings,

They exaggerate every thing.

The picture they paint occupies a big

Screen.

Men nonchalantly brag about themselves,

Male progeny is considered indispensable.

Generally every couple wants a son as heir.

A daughter is considered an outsider.

This mind set influences her upbringing.

She occupies a second place in the scheme of things,

With this suffocating back drop,

How can you accept her in any top slot?

The world is, however, gradually letting a daughter,

Have the same treatment as a son.

Be physically strong, confident, educated and even blunt.

Women all over the world, realistically speaking

Don't always get to do what they want.

The percentage of progressive women must increase,

Men shouldn't be allowed to do what they please.

Despite all social restrictions, daring women have

Entered every field.

Do I still wish to be a man?

An emphatic no, man !

34

Money crunch is always felt.

As you spend more and save less.

Your needs multiply with your status.

You still managed when you earned less.

Why is it that there is no end to spending?

Why can't you control your urge to keep on shopping?

The list of your necessities and luxuries goes on and on.

If you had a 29 inch TV,you want now 44.

Your new refrigerator, kitchen gadgets

Your micro oven, washing machine go beyond your

Budget.

Your style quotient goes up a few notches.

Earlier you wore only ethnic dresses.

Now you eye only branded goods.

Tops, T-shirts, Jeans, suits or shoes.

You never fancied going out often to restaurants.

Now either you order take out food or visit,

Different Oriental or European food haunts.

You used to diligently cook food for a dinner party,

Now you take out your guests too for a treat.

You have chucked a healthy life style.

Your precious time is spent on your medical files.

You send your children to high end schools.

You drive to work in your own car, instead of joining

Car pools.

It is below your dignity to live in a small house.

You keep hunting to own a bigger house to feel proud.

Apparently you have all the trappings of a moneyed man.

But you keep feeling the money crunch again and again.

There is no end to desires.

They pull you deep into the mire.

Why not balance you life?

Earn well,plan well to keep a fairly good life style.

35

Education is a continuous process.
You learn all the time to make progress.
Formal learning takes place in school or college.
You are then young and impressionable.
If you have quality education in a good school,
You learn your basics soon.
Graduating to higher education,
Your knowledge takes you to higher stations.
You choose your career according to your aptitude.
That brings about some status and attitude.
There is some stability around.
You think about having a spouse.
There is an easy transition to adulthood.
Life runs smooth, you feel good.
The scenario changes if instead of good education
You are neglected for many reasons.
Your poor parenting, poverty,
Lack of education and village community.
Prevent you from learning languages, other
Subjects and skills.
In a country where English occupies a pride of place,
Such children lag behind in the race.
Getting opportunities as adults to learn,
A skill or the English language becomes difficult.
Instead of 'she 'they say 'see',

Instead of 'easy' they say 'eajy'.

They take more time to understand any subject.

Still, they are lucky to a get a chance to study that.

Our leaders should give priority to education.

No child should stay uneducated in the nation.

Children will grow up without any complexes.

Their life would be on track without any stresses.

36

Your world goes upside down,
If there is power failure in town.
You can't switch on the AC,
You run helter skelter feeling uneasy.
Your forehead gets dotted with sweat.
Tension gives you palpitating headache.
You want to wash your dirty linen,
The washing machine has no current.
You can't use any electronic device,
The kitchen seems to be very quiet.
100% power back up is provided in flats,
With all the generators spewing sooty smokey spat.
A poor inverter cannot provide much relief.
You must have a generator to have electricity.
That's the only saving grace.
To survive in this place.
Forget about pollution.
That is the government's funeral.
Unless your city gets the smart city tag.
You won't have comforts in your bag.

37

She peeped out of the window,
As if waiting for someone close.
A motor bike thundered past,
Their glances hurriedly met at last.
He wanted to convey a message.
What did he want to say?

She was engaged to be married.
She couldn't change her mate.
Her faith in her family's choice,
Was genuine and true to a point.

Yet she had fallen for this man.
How and when she couldn't tell then.
Just attraction of a kind,
Gradually gripped her mind.

Somehow they managed to meet.
He didn't encourage her to retreat.
Wishing her good luck he disappeared.
She felt as though she was jilted.

He stood in a corner looking longingly at
Her.

When she went through her wedding.
Rituals.
Tears in her eyes she bade him good bye.
God plays with your emotions sometimes,
Handles you like a toy.

You can't indulge in drama all the
While,
Real life is real life.
It mars or makes your life.
If you have courage you break free.
Or continue to suffer, don't flee.
If you do, you give a chance to yourself.
Whether it leads to happiness or failure.
Once your life is disrupted.
Lot of time is wasted.
It is difficult to put it back on track.
Families suffer,it makes you sad.
It impacts your future,
Life can't turn back.
Something or other it lacks.
Moral of the story is,
Think twice before you marry.
Don't jump into matrimony in a hurry,

38

You came into my life,

Like a breath of fresh air.

Your innocent looks,

Your sweet way of speaking,

Your polite manners,

Your naughty demeanour,

Your shining cheeks,

Your cascading black hair,

Your simplicity,

Your undeclared love for me,

Had an effect on me.

I wondered if I was fit enough for you.

With your perfect figure,

Your winning ways.

You were outstanding.

Would you really go along with me?

I wanted life long commitment.

If you could accept me as I was.

A not so well to do man.

A not so handsome man.

A man who loved you though,

Would take care of you all along.

Go to any length with you.

To give you a life of comfort,

And stay faithful and true.

I wasn't sure if you would say 'yes.'
But you accepted my proposal,
And made me the happiest man.
We'll marry with our parents' blessings,
And go for our honeymoon to exotic places.
Marriage shouldn't be the end of love,
It should strengthen day by day.
You should grow old together.
The passion may not stay for ever,
But love and companionship should,
Sweeten your old age.
Memories enrich your days.
Show continuity in your ways.
You stay in love always.

39

Often your mind plays hide and seek.
You hit on a brief wedge quite sleek.
Contemplating on the precious memory,
You wonder if it impacted your story.
A dive into the ever widening memory bank,
You retrieve the most memorable prank.
How your wit and humour attracted some one.
How the spark ignited some soulful connection.
An understanding of a kind was perceived.
Some wave lengths crossed each other immediately.
It was purely intellectual connectivity.
But it touched your sense and sensibility.
An amused expression touched his eyes.
It broadened into a bright smile.
Is that how souls accidentally unite?
It was a parameter of brain activity.
Like minded people merge briefly.
Such Interaction is sure a treasure.,
Giving you a certain pleasure.
It is often a singular episode.
It ends soon being in a fragile mode.
Yet it makes a mark in your life.
It is deleted by and by from your mind.
Going back to that incident once in a while,
Brings involuntary chuckles and smiles.

Mind is the best part of your being.
It gives meaning to breaths you breathe.
You needn't have a body to match.
Your beautiful mind is the best catch.
Wouldn't it be nice, if you clicked with someone.
Before you made up your mind to marry.
Unfortunately you can't forcibly create a click.
You click with somebody somewhere.
You can't force click just anyone any where.

40

Usually people pray at a certain time,
Early morning or late at night.
Often they go to a temple,church or a mosque.
Or have mini home versions of these spots.
The prayers have some preloaded hymns.
They are just sung in tune or rhythms.
Saying these prayers calms the mind.
It pays to remember God at all times.
I offer prayers regularly at night.
But there are so many occasions I need to pray.
When somebody goes out,
I pray that they remain safe and sound.
When somebody falls sick,
I promptly pray for their well being.
When we go out for dinner,
I pray that the food is agreeable.
When I cook something at home and
Inadvertently put some spice in excess,
I keep reciting a very potent prayer,
To help family like the taste of what I have prepared.
When I buy and wear a new dress,
I pray that my husband is impressed.
When I am stressed out and want to relax,
I just pray that I am left to myself.

Infact my prayers go on and on.
I need to pray all day long.
It is a safety ploy.
It brings me lot of joy.

41

She was a pretty lass.
Petite and fair,
She had shining black hair.
We often met at the bus stop,
Between Chandini Chawnk and Red Fort.
Both while going to college or back.
Although we studied in different colleges,
We became quite friendly with each other.

She would tell me that she lived alone.
A town 200 kilometres away was her home.
She visited her family once a month.
She lived as a tenant in Lajpat Nagar.

One day she was not seen on her journey back.
Next morning I tried asking her about that.
She confided in me that she had a boyfriend.
They had been out on a date.

My curiosity got the better of me.
I wanted to know more about him.
She was a bit hesitant to tell me more.
I didn't put any pressure on her any more.

She often began to miss her bus home.
I assumed either she was not in town,

Or she was busy going out with him more often.
One fine day she did show up,
She looked festive and dressed up.
She gave me the good news.
She had married her beau.
I felt happy for her and congratulated her.
She thanked me and soon got into her bus.

She just disappeared from the scene.
I almost forgot that we used to meet.
Suddenly she was spotted again,
As bright as ever she put up a good face.
She seemed happy with her new found
Status.
But continued to stay at her old address.

She,however, told me something I couldn't digest.
Her husband was already a married man.
His wife was illiterate and lived in a village.
He was a lecturer and much older than her.

It was indeed a shock to me.
Why did she go in for a man like him.
Love happened after he wooed her constantly.
She was now married happily.

Well,they were both happy,
So I didn't have to worry.
They will handle their problems,

When they come.
Right now they were happy as a twosome.

He would often take her to five star hotels for dinner.
She had also become an adhoc lecturer.
She enjoyed being pampered.
Never for once regretted her decision.
I was satisfied to see their happiness.

One day after a few months,
I was reading the news paper.
Suddenly an obituary caught my eye.
It was a picture I could identify.
It was my dear friend at the bus stop.
She had passed away a few days ago.

No details were given about her death.
A young charming woman was dead.
It was unpalatable.
But I had no way to find out the truth.
Tears flowed copiously from my eyes.
For a very dear friend who had died.

I wish I had known her more closely,
To advise her not to go in for such an idiotic marriage.
Destiny takes you to unknown shores.
You do not know much for sure.

The mystery of her death still haunts me.

I only hope she wasn't a victim of her husband's family.

May God give peace to her soul and strength to her family.

I will always remember her warmly.

42

Your soul radiates your self.
You rise above everything else.
It is like a halo around your face.
Giving you a frame of grace.
Life turns around 360°
You feel so fresh and free.
No stresses bother you.
It is peace and tranquillity that touches you.
You want to meditate,
Stay quiet and sit straight.
Your eyes look inwards.
See something but can't describe in words.
It is a feeling beyond expression.
Your self undergoes transformation.
Everything inside is so quiet,
Peaceful, joyful and pious.
When you come out of this state,
You feel strengthened and great.
Ready to face the world of day today.
Recognise the fact that God has granted,
You a soul.
It is the better part of your mould.
Avoid negativity,stay in a positive mode.
Life will be fine.
You will continue to shine.

43

Why don't I ever get bored?
It is a problem with most folks.
They go to any length to get rid of boredom.
They play Sudoku, Chess or Candy crush.
Read a book, catch a movie or play tennis,
Go to weekend picnics or card parties.
I do not take the escape route.
I like to bake,steam or cook.
Decorate or redo the interior of my home,
Get new sofa covers, dinner set or
Chopping board.
Go to the tailor to get new suits made,
To get my hair styled or eyebrows shaped.
Go to the bank to withdraw cash,
Buy Tee shirts, towels, shrugs or sash.
Browse through the latest best sellers,
Get junk jewellery to match my dresses.

Make all those calls pending for days.
Make mango or lemon pickles which family
Takes.
Go visit a sick relative in hospital,
Look for sales at pepper fry.com,
Fab furnish, Flipkart, Snap deal or Amazon.
If I still have time from household chores,

I watch TV, go through Applications galore.

I indulge in creative writing,too.

In an attempt to become famous soon.

There surely is no time to get bored.

If I don't get into anything anymore,

I just take an afternoon nap,

Get up fresh,

Enjoy a cup of tea with snacks.

Friends turn up to chitchat.

There is nothing I want beyond that.

44

Hunger is the most potent feeling
Almost everything originates from it.
Hunger for knowledge,
Hunger for fame,
Hunger for love,
Hunger for hate,
Hunger for food,
Hunger for work,
Hunger for rules,
Hunger for nutrition,
Hunger for friendship,
Hunger for beauty,
Hunger for safety,
Hunger prompted you to go out,
In search of food.
That is how you began to work.
Hunger for affection led you to love somebody.
So marriage was invented.
Development of the world,
Happened because you wanted to live well.
If you are content,
You stay put at home.
The urge to do something,
Takes you to think thoughts.
Man has thus created a wonderful world,

For himself.
Stay hungry,
Stay progressive.
Satiate yourself in every way,
Work towards success all the way.
Life opens all the doors,
To let you in on the secrets to live.
You perpetuate yourself,
Create beautiful progeny.
Extending your territory.
Have hunger to live a good life.
Life will get back to you all the while.

45

Death has often knocked at my door.

But somehow I have dodged it.

Am I strong or is it sheer luck?

Every time there is a burning sensation,

I feel I am going to have heart failure.

My suffering is extended.

But death evades me.

After a while it feels better,

Life goes on as ever.

I ought to thank God,

For giving me life.

But I often feel I should die,

At least my pair of one and a half legs,

Would not bother me again.

I won't suffer from phantom pain,

I won't have to wear one, two or three socks

Under the prosthesis.

And still suffer bruises on good half of my leg and knee.

Life wouldn't impede my progress,

I wouldn't have to depend on others for their protection.

But death doesn't come when invited.

It has a way of catching you by surprise.

Life is no doubt a blessing.

It has given you 101 reasons to live.

But it gives quite a few reasons to die too.

No balancing of the scale is required here.
They say when you are born,
Your death warrant is already signed.
There is,therefore, no need to crib.
It will come when it feels fit.
We ought to think of ways to live well,
Rather than count days before death.

46

You value something when you lose it.

Why must you lose it if it is that precious?

Why?

Because a human being errs.

If he didn't he would be perfect.

And he isn't.

Everybody knows that.

It pays to be careful before you delete something.

Think deeply.

Be aware of what you do.

Mull over the content.

If it isn't important,

Don't save it.

You just got a chance to take out your frustration.

It is cathartic.

So it has served its purpose.

Take care to preserve what you may not have again.

It is absolutely a must have situation.

It is terribly complicated to retrieve something from
Trash folder.

Especially from something which is not a regular device.

Be wise to protect what's yours.

The vested interests will try to decimate you.

Mind over matter,

Mind over heart,

Soul over body,
Choose wisely.
Save your important tracks entirely.
You are playing a game.
Choose white or black.
Your choices make or mar your life.
Save,save,save,save,save,
What you indelibly like.

47

If you have to write your will.
You will normally write about,
Property in your name,
Or money in your bank.
You will mention the names of people,
Who should inherit your assets.
How about dividing your intellectual property?
Your letters to your parents and your siblings,
And their letters to you.
The certificates you have saved for years,
Announcing your degrees, your achievements in
Other fields,
Your albums,
Containing all your pictures since childhood,
Your wedding albums, albums showing
Your friends or colleagues, of VIPs you
Had a chance to be with,
Your autograph book,
Your trophies,your CDs containing records,
Of cultural activities during your tenure in your work place.
Apart from such precious memories.
You could also divide your personal effects.
Your stylish dresses ethnic or western,
Your beautiful costume jewellery,
Your gold or silver ornaments.

Your collection of books and music.
Your well chosen furniture and furnishings,
Your paintings, your decoration pieces.
Your electronic devices,kitchen appliances,
Kitchen goods,
Your designer bedsheets or table cloths.
Tea sets or dinner sets.
Well,well !
Nobody wants such things in a will.
They are just additional perks.
The main things family want,
Are gold, land, house or commercial,
Property.
Why waste time and resources,
On people who have no idea,
What is precious or what is superfluous?
Just make a will which is traditional,
There is a chance you will stay in their memory,
As long as they live.
Some day somebody will surely find,
What you really, really cherish.

48

Women never stop fascinating me.

Especially urban women poor or rich.

The poor don't mind working the whole day,

As assistants or helping hands,

At beauty saloons or petrol pumps.

Even as maids, cooks or hair dressers.

Their utmost desire is to give their family the best,

They work hard sincerely to provide them comforts.

Yet I often hear they are beaten up by their men

Who drink and avoid financial responsibility of the family.

The rich,sophisticated women,

Belonging to upper class usually are emancipated

They not only try to keep their family happy

But also look after themselves.

They are usually employed as teachers, doctors,

Engineers, architects or self employed.

They represent the moneyed class,

As they are also married into socially upper class.

They follow the latest trends in fashion,

They are into interior decoration.

Their homes look elegant and well kept.

They are also into the party circuit,

They join women's clubs of all kinds.

Associate themselves with NGOs or socialize.

As for the middle class women,

They stretch their resources to join the upper class,
But they don't match up to them in various tasks.
Women have a keen desire to shine in every field,
In spite of their social standing.
I just never stop wondering at all their skills.
Women should remain empowered.
It is they who keep the family and the nation together.

49

Caste politics, caste marriages, caste reservations,
Are being perpetrated in our country,
If we promote casteless society,
We can dismantle this caste pyramid
We should devise a plan to help the weak,
Our communities will have more teeth.
Education should take precedence over everything.
The government should take over the education scene.
Why should private schools fleece parents?
Quality education should be given free to children.
It would definitely have an impact on the nation.
Higher education or skill training will fill the gap,
Between the have-nots and the haves.
When caste system is annihilated,
There wouldn't be protests to be taken in OBC.
Citizens would have fixed minimum wage,
To survive even when they haven't secured a placement.
Good education would lead to greater employment,
Nobody would complain about being neglected.
First name should be enough to identify a person.
His economic status will be visible to every one.
It will improve his prestige and status in society.
His caste would have absolutely no impact on his personality.
A secular country should allow religions to coexist in peace.
Similarly your caste shouldn't get too much attention in

Society.

Imagine having a chest number instead of a name,

As in the NCC,SSB, Police, Paramilitary or NDA.

That is a brilliant idea to apply instead of using your surname.

The citizens can call themselves with any first name,

They would organize themselves better that way.

Instead of Pan Numbers, Aadhar cards or

Driving licence for ID,

Just know your number to flaunt your identity.

Like car numbers, they can choose their favourite numbers.

All along they would be known as their chest numbers.

Why can't our decision makers think of such plans.

They probably don't want to lose their vote banks.

They deliberately create confusion among the masses.

Democratic society leads a life which nobody trashes.

Equality, liberty,dignity, honesty, sovereignty and freedom,

Are the hallmarks of good governance for any party.

Their agenda should touch the folks of all the classes.

We pray to God,good sense prevails among our leaders,

So that our country and the country men command respect.

50

What is your comfort zone?
Your place of work or your home.
I guess for every one home is home.
Nothing replaces it.
But is it really a comfortable place?
Sometimes you have control over your space.
Sometimes another member of your family,
Has the control buttons.
You want to replace some pieces of furniture,
But you don't do anything of the sort.
For fear you might displease other folks.
Every one can have his own car or bedroom.
But they cannot have different living rooms.
Common consent is needed to bring about changes.
Your comfort zone stays uncomfortable.
Women are given the reigns of the house.
But their men folks have the veto power.
Their word is command.
You try your feminine tricks to buy what you want.
Sometimes you manage,
Sometimes you do not.
You surrender and stay quiet.
But your mood is spoilt.
You get the feeling things are not under your
Control.

Willy nilly you follow the protocol.
You try to feel at home in your own house.
But somewhere you spirit is quashed.
How can you then call your home a comfort zone.
You stay confined to your bed room,wash room
And the dining room.
They are comfortable enough for your volatile
Moods.
They give you a feeling of comfortable home.
You do not really crave for comfort zone.
You have to accept whatever the situation as your
Comfort zone.

51

Women are stronger than men.

They have the capacity to outwit them.

They show tremendous resilience,

They adapt themselves to every situation.

They suffer silently if abused, slapped or tortured.

Their family comes first when they prioritize

Stuff.

Even though humiliated, deprived or turned out,

They think of the prestige of their family through out.

With time unhappy memories are mitigated.

They do not refer to them until reminded.

Past for them is gone.

Future is still to come.

Present is all they like to make better.

They live moment by moment,

Cherishing the best of the moment.

They secure their future,

After having suffered all their life.

They love to make the present worth while.

They always adjust, always compromise.

Their sharp instincts support their mind.

They face ups and downs,

Ignoring the roller coaster rounds.

Stabilise the speed of life.

Control the damage done already,

Men on the other hand do things blatantly,
Damaging themselves and the family.
Reckless, thoughtless, heartless and unsteady,
They go ahead with their adventures nonchalantly.
Often they regret what they did,
Some times it is too late to correct things.
It is women who again come to the fore,
Save the situation taking the right course.
God please multiply the women force,
If you want men to live more.
By themselves they are weak.
With a woman around,
They feel stronger.
Prove me wrong.
I am ready to kneel before you all,
If what I claim is dismissed as false.

52

The prospect of living up to hundred,
Sounds exciting.
If life goes on like this,
I will have to tweak it a bit.
I'll have to think of some tricks,
To get into the groove and jig.
May be I can go in for a face lift.
Reduce my weight a bit.
To look young and fit.
To be honest,age is grace personified.
We automatically give regards to old men and
Women alike.
But I strongly feel we should try to stay healthy.
We should also learn to manage our money.
Have a house of our own,
A personal attendant to see us over,
To help us live with dignity.
One way to have a good time is to stay busy.
Do your own cooking as long as you can.
Wash your clothes,drive,shop and plan.
Invite friends and relatives to dine with you.
Or go out with you,
To see a movie, a play or buy books.
Indulge in creative pursuits.
Like Origami, Paper Mache or Writing a book.

Keeping in touch with your friends,
Who are more or less your age,
Helps you stay connected and safe.
Play Sudoku, solve cross word puzzles or play cards,
It keeps your mind active and smart.
Alzheimers doesn't touch you,
If mental acrobatics is routine with you.
It is when people give up the desire to shine,
That they begin to steadily decline.
Go have a good time,
Shop, sing or dance, go sight seeing,or dine.
Life will go charmingly fast.
Time will fly,you will have a blast.
Do complete a century at least.
Say sayonara and give a birthday treat.
Your smiles with twinkles in your eyes,
Might grant you a few more years of your life.
Live it up !
Radiate joy until your life is done.

53

Whenever I get a call from you,
My BP jumps up to the roof.
My heart beats gallop fast,
I feel I am going to faint and fall.
My excitement knows no bounds.
I get the feeling you are around.

Why has love so much impact on you?
Why can't you stay calm and cool.
Your eagerness to meet your love,
Exceeds any other emotion on Earth.

Once I begin to chat on mobile,
I lose track of time.
Sweet nothings from your mouth,
Are food for my soul which frets around.

O my beloved stay by me a while.
I am going to be thine.
You are my destination in life.
I long for you all the time.

54

I wish to take a dive in the deep pool of your eyes.
The treasure I find in them is difficult to describe.
How could I have lived without you?
I didn't know the taste of love brew.

I draw my sustenance from this potion.
It gives me a thrill beyond notion.
Your warm embrace in chilly winter,
Works better than any electronic heater.

My love for you is beyond superficial warmth,
It stirs emotions from the depth of my heart,
My life would be as dry as a desert.
If you were to leave my life for ever.

Your promises sound very genuine.
I know you will never leave me.
How lucky of me to have you in my life!
We'll be together forever and a night.

55

A shoe shine boy,
Sits on the foot path,
Waits for foot falls close by.
A vegetable vendor,
Goes round the colony.
He is stopped by housewives,
Who generally don't drive.
A delivery boy is a common sight,
He delivers groceries and food on a bike.
A courier also knocks at the door,
Bringing nicely packed goods at every floor.
Young boys on autos are seen,
Delivering newspapers or magazines.
Girls from beauty parlours come home
To cut or dye your hair, apply face packs,
Thread your eye brows,upper lip or wax.
Maids come to cook, wash and clean.
Young men come to teach yoga, or pilates.
Some give acupressure, reflexology or physiotherapy.
Salesmen promote their company's products.
Some sell insurance covers for accidents or
Treatment at hospitals.
There are insignificant small start ups,
Willing to send you trained plumbers, painters,
Maids or drivers.

Every man or woman has a wide choice

To take up some skill based work.

Just look around, you will find,

Men and women self employed or employed for a salary.

At least they live with dignity,

Holding their head high maintaining their prestige.

We should, therefore, pity those,

Who refuse to work and just kill time.

They do nothing but eat,sleep, breed,

And become fat as a toad.

They are a burden for the family,

They are a burden on the nation.

Who will wake them up from this inertia?

I wish some body motivates them

To have self worth and self respect.

Instead of depending on others

They should do just about anything to survive.

That's the only band wagon they should ride.

56

Whenever it thunders,

Lightening strikes,

I begin to shiver,

I feel I might die.

It is reminiscent of a black day in my life.

The world around me rattled.

I was ousted from the cosy comfort of my cocoon.

Illusions often disrupt the peace of your existence.

What you may not have ever thought happened.

Taking away a chunk of your dear life.

A humongous chunk at that.

Your world shook up,

Leaving you bereft.

You were neither dead nor fully alive.

Wake up my little soul.

Belittling doesn't get digested.

There is a limit to being pushed around,

Manipulated, duped,maligned, abused,

Physically and mentally both.

Dragged annihilation sucks.

Dragging you into the pits.

Should or shouldn't you use your wits

To break free of this net of deceit?

The choice between the deep sea and the devil.

Leaves you stumped.

Looking for the lost kingdom.

No human experience comes handy.

Life is crazy.

At least you are alive.

There is nothing that you can't retrieve.

Just try your best.

Don't panic.

The static will die down.

You will wear the winning crown.

57

There was once a little squirrel.

She was fond of the tree she lived under.

She would climb up and down the tree.

She did it with so much ease and expertise,

That you felt she belonged there.

Watching her was a pleasure.

Often she was joined by another squirrel.

May be it was a he seeking a partner.

I never saw anything unusual but soon,

There were baby squirrels!

How the world continues to enrich itself.

So many creatures breed and extend their kind.

God sees to it that there is a cry of little lives.

In his eyes every animal has a right to survive.

If there were only men and women,

It would be a pretty cut and dried kind of a world.

Pups, kittens, cows,buffalos, pigeons and crows,

Elephants, horses, lions,zebras, monkeys or boars,

All will be missed terribly by us.

God in his wisdom strikes a balance,

So that mankind has a better existence.

Man is supreme.

He rules the Earth.

Therefore he knows its worth.

Man has lived like a lord.

He must thank God.

He improves his image everyday.

He has to prove that he is the best.

Outsmarting other living species,

He continues to assert himself.

But the innocence and honesty

Other creatures show

Is something he cannot claim, though.

The world is full of cheats.

There are those who are full of deceit.

I have yet to see animals with extra dimensions.

They are wild by default.

They get aggressive when they feel threatened.

They have survival skills.

They have instincts.

They do not plan wars.

They do not make bombs.

Man though apparently civilized,

Indulges in power games,

Kills for supremacy, pleasure or revenge.

If people lived for love, compassion and justice,

There wouldn't be any war but peace.

The little squirrel is a symbol of peaceful living.

My joy knows no bounds to see her frolicking.

58

Everyday I resolve to fight for my dignity.

But survival forces me to retreat.

Being a woman has its pitfalls.

You cannot win it all.

You postpone taking a stand.

The shaky ground under you will never stabilize.

You in this life would continue to be traumatized.

Tall claims of women empowerment are fake.

She remains tied with chains at the stake.

She tries her best to avoid the bait.

But time and again she falls a prey.

Why is life so difficult for her?

Every now and then she vows to bring about a change.

She has to make her presence felt.

She has to be in the public eye.

If she really wishes to change her life.

It is painful to break your silence.

You wish to condemn violence.

Being heard is a tough task.

Men side with men.

Not much thought is given to women.

As a professional she might shine.

But at home she is just a wife.

She is supposed to remain dumb.

Even if she is vey bright.

A wife sits on a lower rung.

She may have conquered the public domain.

But there is a' Mrs 'before her name.

Which carries the burden of her pain.

59

Remembering you takes me back,
I am in a happy space and track.
It was nothing short of a miracle.
I should run into a dream figure.

The urge to see you was strong.
It was so irrational and wrong.
But I wanted you madly,
Such longing wasn't ever recorded in my memory.

Love is born and reborn much like us.
It is timeless and touches everyone of us.
Social sanction is not a part of this deal.
It comes insidiously from the back gully.

You are romantically and musically inclined.
There is nimbleness in your steps and mind.
Your feeling lost attitude is visible clearly.
You are a gone case, obviously.

This phase is all dream stuff.
It does not last much.
You are back to being normal.
Love is fleeting for mortals.

60

My body fills a slot in space.

I do make a difference,

Just by being myself.

You cannot unseat me by playing tricks with me.

Try outwitting me.

I'll give you back in kind.

You may mind.

I forget,you live more on instincts.

You can never make up your mind.

I mean where it matters.

Anyway, I survive on my own steam.

Whether you approve or disapprove,

I have built up a life for me.

I have used my time to enrich my lot.

I fit a certain slot.

No regrets.

No back track.

My stride is more sure.

I move forward clearing my way.

Obstacles do not deter me.

I try my best to overcome them.

That I survive is proof enough.

I have made a success of my life.

You may have put the lid on me.
But you couldn't quash my spirit.
It has raised me to a certain height.
It has made me luminous like a meteorite.

61

I never knew even pain can be phantom.
It follows after a limb is lost at random.
The stump of your leg feels like a weighty brick.
It gives you jitters to feel the pins and needles.
Your foot lies trapped inside the stump.
It doesn't get moved even if you jump.
The constant awareness of a jammed lid,
Makes you feel queasy, uneasy and unfit.
Rehabilitation is a farce.
They just put you to sleep fast.
You have to fight your own battle.
You have to control all that rattle.
Either you stay busy doing something,
Or you control your thoughts and feelings.
Either way it is your funeral.
Doctors concerned get vicarious pleasure,
Out of performing the procedure on you.
They pocketed a hefty sum to amputate you.
Even after a year and a half, It hurts,
It keeps pricking like a dart and a cut.
If you go to the surgeon,he excuses himself.
He has to go to the OT,
To do the same operation on others.
An assistant looks you up and down,
"Dearie, you have to handle it on your own.

We can't do much except give you depressants.
You have to accept that you are handicapped.
The phantom pains are universally known.
As soon as we know more we'll inform you on phone."
"Get lost now," he mutters in an undertone.
I feel lost. Where shall I go now?
Who shall I plead with?
I have to be brave and manage.
I have to put up with this madness.

62

Out of the box,

Or inside the box,

All thoughts occupy space on top.

Sometimes you save what you hear or speak

Sometimes you don't.

But years later you recall an event in some context.

Memory recalls are amazing.

I wonder why I can't recall examination stuff.

Yet I had passed those exams.

Memory is selective.

You register what you learn as a lesson in life,

Or what then was important, generally speaking.

The rest is forgotten.

Funny,isn't it?

Human mind is complex.

Thinking is a natural process.

You analyse and sum up.

Take decisions and move forward.

This is an intelligent way of going about life.

Dull brains must be brushed up,

To avoid Alzheimers.

Mind under control leads to prosperity.

You don't waste your money recklessly.

Stay alert, active and caring.

Live life enthusiastically.

63

What is work ethics?

Work sincerely,yes.

Arrive on time, yes.

Update your knowledge about your work, yes.

Stay on friendly terms with colleagues, yes.

If you have to do overtime, do it if paid for it, yes.

Introduce innovative techniques to fast track work, yes.

Let the chief know what you do, yes.

Seek his approval if required, yes.

Please the boss, yes and no. Yes as you have to show

Efficiency. No, not in any personal way.

You are not obliged to do personal things for him, yes.

Don't go shopping with him, yes

Don't get physical with anybody, yes

If you fall in love with somebody,

If the other person also feels the same way,

Arrange to meet somewhere else in your own time, yes.

It is unfortunate but it doesn't

Happen that way,

After all you are human.

Discretion is needed in such situations.

Don't make a spectacle of yourself.

Work ethics demands objectivity.

As far as possible official work should be strictly official.

Clean and hygienic atmosphere begets quality work.

Be ethical in your work place.

If you want to work satisfactorily.

You get paid just for your work.

Decent behaviour counts.

Everybody wants a break to relax.

Organise group activities to loosen up a bit.

Get back to work refreshed and active.

Falling for somebody is not a crime per se.

But mixing it with work is bad practice.

It is you,you and you alone who decides what to do.

It is your call. You call the shots.

Save your job or save your contacts or both.

64

Swashbuckling, adventurous, fun loving,

Sunny side always up, witty and humorous,

Generous, giving, charming, understanding,

Suave, chivalrous,dapper, good looking.

Such individuals are a rare phenomena.

They impress almost all upscale young women.

They don't mean to but often they flirt.

Innocent sweet nothings are often taken seriously.

Poor,poor men, they get entangled unwittingly.

They have to back track judiciously.

Often it is difficult to do so.

You break hearts.

As you can't pretend to love someone,

When you don't.

You are in a fix.

Get out or stay in.

Both ways you lose.

You earn a bad reputation if you act mean.

Why not just face it.

Say it was all a misunderstanding.

It is a gentlemanly way of retreating,

If you don't want to be called a cad,

Go ahead and snub the woman rudely.

All your life this guilt will take you down in your own
Esteem.

The woman will be disillusioned.

She will probably never trust any man.

In her eyes most men will be cads.

Men,think before you get involved.

Don't mislead anyone into thinking you love.

Check it if somebody acts as if in love with you.

Nip it in the bud.

Stop being a dud.

65

Instant noodles,
Instant coffee.
Instant money,
Instant honey,
Instant luck,
Instant buck,
Instant food,
Instant good,
instant light,
Instant fight.
Instant matter,
Instant chatter.
Instant colour,
Instant butter.
Instant nirvana.
Instant fame.
Instant name.
Instant recovery.
Instant death.
Instant culture is in vogue.
Is it quantity over quality?
It is a way of getting fast results.
Some like it some don't.
You can't help getting affected.
You want to stay in touch with it.

Try it.
Reject or love it.
Stay cool.
Why crib?

66

I love being at home.

I am not an extrovert.

I love my own company.

I seldom get bored.

Having given a well balanced meal to my family,

I feel content as a housewife,

I take an afternoon siesta.

Sleep like a log.

Dream of my childhood and youth

Indigenous games take me back to childhood,

In summers we slept in the lawn outside our flat.

Played together as if there was no worry in the world.

A religious occasion used to be a family affair.

Now just my counterpart and I celebrate it.

Change is the only constant.

By and by life turns upside down.

It happens so insidiously.

You hardly realise you have changed.

The young jolt you into the present,

When they address you as they do a grand parent.

Forever young is a myth.

Forever happy is just a state of mind.

Being stress free is living in the kingdom of yore.

You cannot duplicate that status any more.

67

What makes a day for an ordinary person.

Going for a walk?

Getting a good breakfast?

Working 9 to 5?

Comfort of public transport?

Enjoying a cup of tea with family?

Helping the children do home work?

Playing with them?

Enjoying dinner at home?

Well,these things are routine.

He doesn't even notice these comforts.

He takes them for granted.

His day is made when he gets a raise,

When he takes his family out for dinner.

When his son shows brilliant results.

When his wife gets a make over to his liking.

When he watches a cricket match and his country wins.

When he buys a high end car.

When his house gets a fresh paint.

These things are not really out of the ordinary.

But then he is an average citizen.

You don't expect him to get a Nobel Prize.

You don't expect him to go on a world tour.

He remains a down to earth citizen.

He is reasonably happy with his lot.

Even if he is not, what can one do?

Weave a magic wand?

Turn him into a rich lord?

No way.

A common man remains a struggling man.

68

She is obsessed with her looks.
When she buys branded goods,
She has to return them at least twice,
Before she decides they look nice.
A huge mirror is absolutely a must.
It helps her with her hourly make up.

Aging is sometimes clearly noticed,
But admiring yourself is needed.
It enhances your confidence.
Your looks do matter.
You impress with your sense of style
Your wit and humour add a mile of smile.

Being socially active is necessary.
It gives you a purpose to carry.
You show your talent,your ideas,
If you work for social causes.
You help the weaker sections.
You rise up the social ladder.

Being well dressed and presentable counts.
You radiate smartness when you go around,
You attract big shots and well known folks.
Your circle of friends gets wider as you become

Bold.
Dear woman, your persona gets quite charming,
Page 3 becomes yours for the asking.

So never compromise on improving your image.
It is through and through an advantage.
Combined with you talent,it takes you far.
You not only impress bigwigs but stay at par.
God helps those who help themselves.
Learn to keep your morale high,
You have learnt the ropes to continue to be bright.

69

Why should demented men be allowed to marry?
They are a problem to themselves and society.
A poor innocent woman is sacrificed in marriage to
Him.
Living her whole life in terror,humiliation,violence,
And degradation.
She survives on her common sense and her salary,
Being a working woman.
Her health both mental and physical suffers.
For fear of family outrage you are taken to a
Hospital when a serious health issue comes up.
But ground reality doesn't change.
He continues to torture the poor woman by putting
Her down even when she is hospitalised.
She is educated, fairly good looking.
She belongs to a well to do and cultured family.
There is no history of abuse and violence in her
Family.
It is all the more difficult for her to tolerate such
Demeaning behaviour.
Dear friends,what do you suggest she should do?
Give him up and live alone.
Her concern is she doesn't have the strength to
Survive alone.
Her life has always remained under wraps.

Let it remain as it is.

Let her suffer indignities.

In the eyes of the world she is legally married.

Isn't that a reward of the best kind for the lady?

70

There is a manicured park in my colony,
Teeming with young and the old cronies.
They chat incessasntily about topical news,
Critisizing right and left the leaders new.
It makes them feel better,
As they can't do any better.
They talk of the rising prices of groceries,
The difficulty of using broken roads by the
Motorists.
Rapes,killings in the name of caste & religion.
Our relationship with the neighbouring nations.
IPL or T20 cricket matches in and around their city.
Yearly festivals which cause traffic jams,
Pollute the local river and surrounding lands.
Women talk of recipes, fashion and their in-laws.
Men stick to stocks and shares, politics or wars.
The elderly talk about their ailments or hospitals.
Children are the happiest lot who play and mingle.
You can see a yoga class going on, some joggers,
Some walkers some walking their dogs.
A park denotes a lively, friendly place.
To exercise, socialise, run, jog or shout at the top.
It serves the purpose of bringing neighbours
Together,
Who usually remain cooped up inside their houses.

There should be plenty of such places,
For citizens to get together and interact with each
Other.
Celebrate festivals which bring joy and cheer.
They probably pay peanuts for maintenance.
Welfare associations must be strengthened,
To bring about quick repairs,law and order,
Adequate supply of water, electricity and upkeep of
Roads and gardens.
We must own the responsibility of being a citizen.
If we feel proud of our nation.

71

On line shopping is so much fun.
Nobody disturbs you when you look up,
For the endless choices in clothes,shoes, jewellery,
Electronics, kitchen goods, books and grocery.
You just place your order and track it on the given
Numbers.
You don't hop from shop to shop in retail outlets,
Have street food for lunch, a Coke or Pepsi for
Water.
You don't have to travel in crowded metro.
Carry a heavy bag for God knows how much
Shopping load.
Walk through crowded roads,
Haggle over prices of the stuff you bought.
God forbid if you have to return something to
Exchange,
You go through the same exercise all over again.
Long live on line shopping.
There is nothing more attractive.
However there is a flipside too.
If you don't happen to like the stuff you receive,
You have to keep the tags intact,pack the stuff,
And call them to collect the packet with invoice.
If they accept the complaint, your money goes to
Your bank.

You don't get it back in your hand.
It is no doubt a hassle.
Buying from markets or malls is hectic,
But it gives you pleasure to buy first hand,
Technology has made things more convenient.
More and more people are going in for on line
Shopping.
Progress dear friends, progress.
Catch the habit of shopping while at rest.

72

She is grace personified.
With salt and pepper hair and dignified.
Knitting was a hobby with her.
She made sweaters and jerseys for her family.
She was always seen with a book in her hand.
She was an avid reader of best sellers at hand.
A chatterbox that she was she won friends easily.
Whenever there was a cricket match she
Concentrated on the commentary excitedly.
She had a thin book describing fundas of Civics.
She had learnt the entire text by heart to teach.
Nobody could guess that she was almost sixty.
She spread her charm around in company.
She clicked with me as we both loved books.
We read books in free time in the library or the
Nooks.
I admire folks who are into reading books of all
Genres.
They may read fiction, biographies, motivational books or
pamphlets.
The written word retains charm all of its own.
There is no comparison with any other form.
I don't remember too many people I have worked
With.

But I seldom forget colleagues who shared books
With me.
When studying literature we quoted poets and
Dramatists at the drop of a hat.
We played with words and found punning the best.
You seldom find people who are on the same wave
Length.
You go through life mingling with dull and boring
People.
I miss my witty and clever with words college
Friends and lecturers.
They contributed to my intellectual growth in
Future.
Thank you friends.I remember you a lot.
I know not where you are,at which hot spot.
But hope to run into you some place in some slot.

73

Memories are like vines around a tree.

They hold you and clutch you, but don't flee.

Their grip is difficult to loosen up or break.

You want to forget some, remember some.

You can't always choose.

Some are nicely wrapped up with stunning steel.

Some are like deep wounds which take time to heal.

You go round and round, just letting time go by.

Filling your mind and heart with daily grind.

Connecting to people is a herculean task.

You might ignore some, encourage some, like or

Don't like all.

You at least pose as a friend or somebody known.

Going beyond is a rare event.

Most people you work with have only work contact.

Once in a life time you might have a crush on

Someone.

For all you know you might already be committed to

Someone.

Memories are built around good times or difficult

Times.

They often cling to you.

No eraser works efficiently to delete them for you.

Most of the weight of your body is stored on the

Stomach.

Do they rest there? I think it is absurd.
The brain, poor thing can't share them with any
Other organ.
Yet it doesn't change its size.
It has a big chip to store everything in your life time.
It is indeed competition for technology.
Brave technocrats, invent something which can add
To its value.
It should have the option to delete what you
Don't want to review.
I would love to have the freedom to remember
Some or forget some.
It will have lot of possibilities.
Sitting for examinations, for one, will not be
Rocket Science.
You will pass with flying colours and rise in life.
You will refuse to recognise people you don't like.
You will remember names all your life.
As you grow old forgetting becomes routine.
Having control over everything, you will not forget
Important things.
You will remember anniversaries and birthdays.
Your friends and family will appreciate this new
Trait.
I can go on and on to write an ode to pleasant
Memories.
But I would rather stop here and go to sleep
Peacefully.

74

Speech can be persuasive.

Keeping mum gives others a chance to be derisive.

The rule: 'Speak when you must'

Works for you but not always with others.

You may write well.

But if you want to impress others,

You must make your presence felt.

Speak up, assert yourself

The way you modulate your voice,

The way you choose your words,

The way you handle the audience,

The way you handle the topic,

Everything makes an impression.

It even gets you compliments.

It contributes to your popularity.

You win friends instantly.

Speaking nineteen to a dozen is debate.

You speak for or against.

It is a different genre of speech.

Just interacting is breaking the ice.

It brings people close for a while.

If you avoid speaking,your expressions say a lot.

If you are listening to someone, their expressions

Convey a lot.

You must go on building your vocabulary.

If you don't know the exact meaning,consult the
Dictionary.
A life long affair with words,
Gives you immense knowledge and satisfaction.
Your life is richer for it.
You handle situations better and make yourself a
Niche.

75

A woman is resilient and down to earth.
She continues to manage the home and the hearth.
She seldom gets any compliments.
She is often snubbed or mocked at.
Treated more like a slave
Even abused or slapped.
She doesn't run away to save her life.
She waits for sense to prevail.
She does not retaliate.
Where does she get this wisdom from?
When there is calm for a while before the next
Storm.
Life goes on without any drastic change.
Others may not sense her pain.
Her family would get bad reputation,
If she reacts to every situation.
Her moral strength is exceptional.
She has cultivated good manners.
If awareness dawns on her,
She will change her stance.
Mould others to follow her glance.
The attitude of men needs to change
Give women credit for keeping them sane.
Progressive or not progressive,
They continue to treat women as a weaker species.

Hence their superior stance in every field.

Women really have to be bold,

Assert themselves in every role.

Just being an annexe to men is demeaning.

Speak up for yourself,

Diplomatically change the scenario.

You have a lot of substance.

Never let anybody short change you.

Never let anybody pull you down.

Let them eventually bow down.

They will definitely come round.

76

Women migrants in some countries,
Especially from Asian countries,
Go through racial bias due to the colour of their
Skin.
Even though holding degrees from prestigious
Universities.
Why are such nations called advanced countries?
They don't even understand what global citizen
Means.
These migrants are ill treated,
Not adequately paid and often insulted.
The local people frown upon their colour,
They underestimate their worth.
The struggle the Asian women undergo to earn a
Living,
Shows their grit and desire to make it in their field.
They don't lose their mental balance,
Continue to overcome the bias against them.
They migrate under pressure.
Financial or personal reasons sometimes force you
To take such decisions.
Given the choice nobody would leave their country.
Ambitions or family problems too bring them to
Face such conditions.
If you belong to a developing country,

To upgrade your status,at times,you go to a
Progressive country.
Experience tells you no migrant has it easy.
She is made fun of, down sized and under
Employed.
It takes a lifetime for her to be accepted as one of
Them.
There are many such stories under wraps in such
Places.
I wish more women come forward to share them
Without any complexes.
They will be noticed and gradually their lot will turn
Better,
Inhuman ways to treat them give a dirty picture of
That nation.
If such issues are brought to the notice of
International Women's Forums,
The lot of migrants will definitely become better.

77

A little bird whispered into my ear.

I want you to fly with me.

You look as if you are lost.

Life's crooked streets have landed you in a spot.

I know not what is going on in your mind.

You badly need a change of scene to feel fine.

Would my way of life please you?

I seldom stay at one place.

I travel all the time.

Fly with me to see the world.

It has charms beyond belief.

I'll show you those places with a bird's eye view.

You will just see prominent land marks.

You will fly past without noticing the troubled spots.

You will lead a comparatively better life,

If you adopt this policy all the while.

I perch on trees to enjoy the ambience.

I feel free to go anywhere.

Do you ever give yourself' me' time?

Are you perennially tied down with work?

Does your family demand all your attention?

You go through a lifelong struggle.

Can you put aside your worries for some time?

Just to reflect on what you really want in life.

I just fly to far off lands to reach the horizon.

I stop when hungry or tired.

In my world we have the freedom,

To do just about any thing.

But flying is my passion.

It is a natural gift.

Try joining me.

Just freak out.

Do anything you please.

Stress-free life is the basic need.

You will fall for my life style.

You may not exactly fly.

Imagine crossing the sea!

Diving to the depth of the ocean.

Discovering millions of sea creatures.

Flying, swimming, driving help you move.

Walk, run, jog help you improve.

Life beyond extinction is unseen.

There is a treasure beyond miles and miles,

Of the sea.

78

Progress and innovation are part of a nation.
A country survives on industries and education.
Technology has changed parameters,
Everything centres around the internet.
You plug in the WIFI as you get up from your bed.
Your day begins with various calls on your mobile.
Your schedule for the day is on Memo or Drive.
On line or off line the mobile serves you day and
Night,
Your computer, MacBook or mobile makes your life
Smarter.
You can book a taxi, order a meal or
Shop for almost anything.
Groceries or medicines, fashion products, electronic
Gadgets, kitchen goods, jewellery, shoes, mobiles or their
Accessories, furnishings or home decor,
Are all within your sight to choose from a stock
Pile.
Very soon you won't need to look up your office files.
Just about everything will be done for you on line.
Service will be available to help you with your
Household chores.
It will help you fix your tap, gas, Zero B, heater,
Fryer, chimney or stove.
You won't need to walk an inch further than your

Door.

You will use your personal elevator down the

Floor.

Your car with GPS will remain on auto pilot,

Just a step outside the car and you are on the

Escalator.

Nobody will be seen around but video conferencing

Will begin.

Brain storming will yield results,

Decisions will be taken.

Your job done.

Buttons will rule the world.

Your fingers may hurt for being overused.

Stylus will be used more often.

Speed wouldn't scare you,

Systems on vehicles will stop them from colliding.

Music will be heard on ear phones alone,

To avoid noise pollution.

Polluted air due to machines around,

Will force people to go around in insulated trolleys,

Gyms will replace parks for free volleys.

My imagination is running overtime,

Before everything turns mechanical,

Let me go out to breathe natural.

Let there be a balance between technology,

And work done by your strong body.

Otherwise you will be back to the future.

79

Destiny holds the reigns of your life.

You wanna go South,

It leads you to North.

It decides,

The career you choose.

Who you marry,

When you marry,

Where you are going to die,

When do you die.

Whether you stay poor or rich,

If you have children,

If you stay without children,

If you are going to lose your limbs,

If you live a heathy life,

If you get addicted to drugs,

If you get a divorce,

If you drink to forget your miseries.

If your children, in turn, live a good life,

If your marriage has negative impact on you,

If you flourish after marriage,

If you get promotions in time.

If you are superseded by your juniors,

If you achieve fame,

If you are suspended at work,

If you commit a crime,

If you rot in jail.

If you have a major accident,

If you are crippled for life.

Destiny is blamed for everything negative in life.

Destiny is credited for your success and luck.

God himself controls your destiny,

But if you believe in your abilities,

You can bring about a change for the better in your

Life.

Work towards your goals,

Destiny will bring you victory.

Do believe in destiny,

But never cease to put in your best,

In everything you do.

Destiny is attracted to such people,

It makes sure that you succeed,

In whatever you do.

80

Sweeping generalisations are often wrong.
All women don't represent every woman.
There are women who are delicate and feminine.
They remain dependent on their men.
They dare not fight for their rights.
But today's young women are made of sterner
Stuff.
They are outgoing, bold, ambitious and assertive.
They know their minds.
They will not take shit from anybody.
A friend, husband, children or their boss.
They chuck their job if exploited or underpaid.
They ask for a divorce if hurt in some way.
Some do get fired for being cheeky.
Women who are docile suffer the most.
Keeping mum for them is a virtue,
They often pile up praise from relatives,
For keeping all abuse under wraps.
After all they do not wash their dirty linen,
In public.
Once married they are wished well by relatives.
Who never really get to know the truth.
Such women suffer silently.
If they speak up, they will be thrashed till they turn
Blue.

Poor women, they accept their lot graciously.
Not sharing their tale with friends or relatives.
God,please let men be a little more
Humane, kind, compassionate and generous.
Women,rise,make some dent somewhere
The world needs to know,
How men perpetrate crime against them.
Treat them rough,
Abuse them,rape them, degrade them,discard
Them.
Just a little vestige of dignity is left in them.
Most just accept their lot.
Some flee or commit suicide.
Some get murdered,some disfigured with acid.
When do women get to live at par with men.
Awareness has to be spread.
NGO 's must help downtrodden women,
Earn their own livelihood.
Make a life of comfort, security and dignity.
Then only there will be semblance of parity and
Equality with men.
It is an unending, uphill task.
Relentlessly we must go on to improve their lot.
Provide them respect and social slots.
Education, housing, jobs are to be created for them.
So that they don't pity themselves.
They hold their head high and live with grace.

81

You often put a mask on your face.

You don't show the harsh reality of your case.

As long as nobody notices,

You carry on with your facade.

The moment it gets known,

You are dubbed a coward.

You invite interest in your circumstances.

People tend to become nosey,

Sometimes even try to help you.

Some even enjoy feeling superior,

Begin to speak in condescending tones.

Why won't they leave you alone?

Sometimes your loss becomes somebody's gain.

They use the situation to their advantage.

We humans are basically self oriented.

We save our skin first, then think of being socially
Effective.

It is practical to love yourself first,

If you are healthy and strong,

You stay fit enough to never go wrong.

Your strategy to save others will be two pronged.

You help bring out others from sticky situations,

You earn a reputation for being bold and
Courageous.

82

You never know when love jumps into your life.

You are caught unawares.

You like being complimented,

You like being the object of somebody's affection.

Yet it is a strange feeling.

It disturbs you.

It misleads you too.

Your life is disrupted.

Your mind becomes clouded.

Your life goes upside down.

Why is it so complicated?

It feels nice.

You are drenched in adralin rushes.

For no fault of yours you are pulled into this mess.

God, I would like to be spared this strange

Experience.

Please keep me away from this untimely attraction.

It doesn't behove a woman of a certain age.

Such chemistry should be a part of your youth.

Life should be divided into phases,

As in Indian philosophy.

Education, work, marriage, children,moving

Towards Spirituality and thoughts of the world

Beyond.

Overlapping of such staggered events is painful.

Some people marry,then get a job.
Some have a baby,then they marry.
Some denounce the world when young.
Some die prematurely.
Some live to remain illiterate,
Lead a life meaningless in ignorance.
Some can't do without going astray though happily
Married or unhappily for that matter.
Why is there so much disparity in this world?
God please put everybody's life in order.
Let things happen in the right sequence,
At the right age.
Please don't deprive individuals of all the stages of
Life.
They remain graceful if they run their tenure
Peacefully, Joyfully and enthusiastically.
Equality, security, sovereignty.
Suitable work, soulmate, children, disease free long
Life is everybody's birth right.
O Almighty,grant every one a life of quality.
I express my deep gratitude in anticipation,
For disbursing such equality.

83

Everybody sports multifaceted persona.
You are bright and cheerful when with friends.
You look glum when faced with your problems.
There is a semblance of glitter in your eyes,
When you achieve something in life.
You dance and chill at a wedding.
You look elegant in your formal clothing.
At home you romp around in tracksuits or casuals.
You wear a tie and suit at work.
Dress apart your moods fluctuate.
You show your temper when rubbed the wrong
Way.
You are tickled when you find something comic.
Your superficial self peeps through your armour,
When you try to play games.
You look foolish when in love.
Sanity is back when you come out of it unscathed.
You put your best foot forward to impress others.
Your real personality comes out when in distress.
Either you break down or show your strength.
You change colours like a chameleon.
If you didn't,
You would be fake.
It is the nature of man to keep on changing his
Stand.

He is casual with friends.

Formal at work.

Non challant with family.

Rude with irritable people,

Joyous with kids.

Soft with women.

Angry when ridiculed.

Happy when content.

He always keeps others guessing,

As he is an expert in being a drama king.

84

Gender stereotype,
Gender equality,
Need to be discussed,
The problem is:
Men wish to be all powerful.
They will not come down from their high horse.
Especially a married man.
He remains supreme for his woman.
She dare not point out his weaknesses.
If she is bold she might confront him.
But she is turned into pulp,
Hit right and left,
Abused and kicked.
If she dares to contradict him.
Crying, her eyes welled up with tears,
She consoles herself that no major harm is done to
Her body.
But cry within deepens into a wound,
Which would not easily heal.
Following the routine she does,
Her household chores.
Life becomes apparently normal.
Gender bender, gender equality,
Are resounding echoes,
Which can be heard miles away,

But nothing happens on the ground.

A woman continues to be tortured.

She has no saviour.

She just has to pray that she dies.

She doesn't expect gender sensitiveness from,

The other gender.

Discussions are banal.

You raise a clamour at public platforms.

You may be given standing ovation.

But don't expect to see any change in your life.

A woman is vulnerable.

She will remain so.

Men will be men.

They will continue to bully women and children.

They are Gods.

Worship them.

Don't talk of gender equality.

This is a lot of hog wash.

Rubbish.

Nobody is equal.

May be on paper.

Yes, but not in reality.

85

Why is everybody so sensitive about aging?
It is so natural.
On observation,
You will accept,
You and all your contemporaries have begun to
Show signs Of age.
You kind of shrink,
Your face tells it all.
You walk with difficulty.
Your energy levels are low.
Still you are game for outings or parties.
You look elegant in whatever you wear.
You feel more free to express yourself.
Everybody feels you are harmless.
Your sunny smiles light up any group of people.
Your advice and tales are often edifying.
Experience is your tool.
If you are side tracked or dismissed
It is not only unkind but stupid.
Your words have more worth and wisdom,
You can be tracked years down the road.
Never let depression overpower you.
Age gracefully.
Your spunk and spirit is visible to all.
Command respect.

Your attitude reveals your strength.

The young dare not ignore you,

Exploit you,

Degrade you,

Snub you,

Snap at you,

Ignore you,

Throw you out of your house.

Be wise enough not to transfer,

All your wealth,land or house,

To your children while you are alive.

Write a will.

It works better.

Change it with time if need be.

Some descendants don't behave themselves.

They begin to be rude or even cruel.

Save yourself and your assets for you and your

Spouse,

Being practical makes the dusk in your life,

Comfortable and safe.

Generosity is good,

But save your skin first.

Love yourself to be able to love others.

Old age is not a curse.

It is time to reflect on mysteries of life and death.

Your victories and failures.

Being spiritual and involving God more in your

Thoughts and prayers with real issues.

Not just requests and safety.
Giving a personal touch to your prayers,
Seeking peace and quiet,
Seeking an easy slide into the other space.
Seeking his presence all along.
Welcome old age.
You will surely be appreciated for your fiery spirit,
Live your life till your last breath.
Take good care of yourself.
God be with you.

86

Fashionistas rule the world's stage.
Actresses and models walk the ramp.
In pajama party wear, gowns and bridal range.
Ethnic suits, skirts,stoles, shawls and pants,
With trendy shoes, head gear and capes.
The young college crowd apes such designs.
I wonder what happens in class or corridors.
Eye candies all around,
How do you pay attention to lectures?
There must be more couples dating each other.
Concentrating on studies must be the second
Option.
Well,your dress gives you a unique identity.
You definitely look good.
It shows your attitude.
It brings out your confidence.
But when in college,
Make the most of your time.
Let your schedule be priortized
Your degree will add to your status.
Your affairs might waste your time
It is only wise to give attention to your subjects.
Being friendly with classmates is enough.
Exchanging notes helps.
Ultimately it is not your wardrobe,

That wins you a placement.
Your score in the finals,
Is what you must aim at.
Post graduate courses are tough.
For higher education,
Your ability in a subject of your choice matters.
Dear girls,have a vision for your future.
Your mission should be to become financially
Independent.
Comfortable wear will do.
Unless you want to be a fashionista,
You want to be noticed.
Make it to Bollywood,
Or conquer the ramp.
Become a fashion designer.
That's all.
Fair enough.
Get trained professionally.
Don't waste your time.
Be ready to face competition.
We wish you all the best.

87

When young and pretty,
Every girl wishes to marry.
She has dreams of a prince charming,
Who would make love to her,
Sweep her off her feet.
He would say sweet nothings to her,
Take her out for candle night dinners.
Honeymoon will be fulfilling,
She would turn into a woman from a girl.
This transformation will be natural.
Life hence would be full of joy.
Together they would build a nest,
Cozy and comfy, full of love.
There will be little ones around.
Life would be completely satisfying.
Well! Well!
What happens is another story.
Your dreams get broken overnight.
He begins to find faults with you.
You have instructions to please every one.
There is no romance as anticipated.
He just goes through the ritual in bed,
As if performing a duty.
There is no tenderness as dreamt of.
It is all awkward and messy.

Generally now onwards you feel lost.

Understanding everything and everybody is

Difficult.

You are reprimanded for slightest oversight.

When alone you cry your eyes out.

You can't complain to anyone.

You feel stuck in a sticky situation.

There is no way to improve matters.

You carry on for fear of ridicule.

A whole life passes by,

You begin to comprehend,

Being married and being happy,

Are mutually exclusive.

Manage if you can.

If you can't,divorce is an option.

Very few women have the guts to do that.

Or be a regular victim of domestic violence.

Compromise you do.

You save yourself from social embarrassment.

Years go by.

Anniversaries are wished.

Nobody tries to discover the truth.

88

She is trapped into a relationship.
Willy nilly she fulfils her duties.
She would like to see the world.
She wants to enjoy chatting with someone.
She wants to laugh.
Gracefully dance a waltz.
Go round and round,
Dreamily touch and feel the ground.
She wants to do up her home
Elegant furniture, stylish decore.
Flowers, T-candles and furnishings,
All must reflect her taste.
She would love to host her friends,
Just to have company which is pleasant.
Go for long,brisk walks to stay healthy,
Chat up with neighbourhood women,
Breathe fresh air and enjoy herself.
She wishes to work to keep herself busy.
Take up some social issue to help society.
She wants to go shopping in malls.
She wants to own things money can buy.
Watch the latest movie from Bollywood,
With colleagues and friends from childhood.
Her desires run amok.
She wishes to own gold, diamonds and silver.

While watching TV programmes and soaps,
She admires interesting plots and reality shows.
She is the kitchen queen.
Enjoys cooking,
Roasting, baking,boiling,salad dressing.
She is fond of music.
She freaks out to hear any old classical melody.
Lyrics,instrumental music or poetry.
She wants to live,
She wants to live it up.
Express herself and never shut up.
Let no one deny her these simple pleasures
She will go on with her life guarding her treasure.

89

When you are old and weak,
You want to relax and read.
You gave your best to your family,
When young and sturdy.
Now that old age knocks at your door.
What do you do to postpone it for sure?
The best thing is to remain fit.
Exercise, go for walks or to a gym.
Eat healthy food and stay happy.
Continue to indulge in your favourite hobby.
Be it cooking, gardening,writing or social work.
If your mind is busy and you do DIYs,
Your day is passed satisfactorily.
If you keep cribbing about your ailments,
Your mood fluctuates, your temper flares.
Going out for shopping with family,
Catching a movie with just about anybody,
Will add fun quotient in your routine.
Dressing up in fashionable clothes,
Being active in sightseeing and sports,
Will give you immense pleasure.
Enjoying company of fellow oldies,
Can take you back to your memories.
Keeping company of young ones,
Provides you fodder for fun.

They are naturally full of joi de vivre.
That makes you feel young.
Anybody who calls you old must be shunned,
You should still be groovy, voguish and elegant.
Celebrate being alive.
It is a beautiful life.

90

Soon you will be married,
Your dream will be realised.
All through your childhood,
You dreamt of a princely groom.
He will be at your door.
To wed you to take you home.
Excitement and an unknown fear,
Give you a mixed feeling.
You anticipate lots of love,
You fear the novelty of wedded love.
How would it happen and when.
You will also face a new family.
You took your parents for granted.
They fulfilled all your demands.
They pampered you no end.
If you were in pain,
Your parents felt your pain.
They treated you as a princess.
They kept you happy in everyway.
If you were late from work,
They waited at the door being very tense.
You were a darling daughter.,
Who brought in their life sunshine and laughter,
Your welfare was paramount to them,
You were precious to them.

Their life centred around you,
And your sister a few years younger than you.
You bonded with each other like twins.
She followed your lead in everything.
Now that you leave her,
She feels the crunch.
Your family now will take a back seat.
You will visit them now and then only.
Life wouldn't be the same again.
Your room won't be yours anymore.
Your belongings will still be there,
Whenever you choose to take them away.
You will now be a part of your new family.
You will be expected to look after everybody.
Tables will be turned on you.
You will have to adjust anew.
Initially they will try their best to make you feel
Welcome.
By and by you might even have your share of fun.
Honeymoon over, you enter the kitchen.
You may know cooking or you may not.
You will try to please all
You are now on your own.
From a vulnerable little girl you are now a
Housewife.
A regular socialite.
Dressed in finery you are on show.
You will begin to feel the pressure on you.

Dear girl,you are inducted into an alien zoo.

Survive,

Or give up and cry.

Call mama and papa or your dear sister

You have to carve your niche for better or worse.

Childhood is over.

The golden period is over.

The pain of parting with your family will remain.

But you will have a lot of things to gain.

We give you blessings to lead a fulfilling life

You are stepping into a new life.

Don't you cry and make every one cry.

You are loved dearly,don't you ask why.

You were the apple of every one's eye.

91

If you hadn't been there,
I wouldn't have met anybody worth the name.
To teach me any craft or skill.
I wouldn't have got a suitable job,
I wouldn't have been good at anything.
I wouldn't have even studied in a prestigious
University.
Even if I did,
I wouldn't have had any command over my subject.
Of course, I should say I owe it to you.
If you hadn't taken me out in your car,
I wouldn't have ever seen my town,
I wouldn't have even been to any restaurant.
I would never have bought any books or music.
I would never have risen in my career but for you.
Friends, you must forgive me,
I am not talking about my parents or my siblings,
Or my husband but somebody close to me who
Likes to believe,
If she hadn't been there I would still be a dunce,
May be illiterate, rustic or good for nothing.
I should go tell her,
Short of giving birth to me,
I am her product,
Or a protégé,

To please her,
To boost her ego.
I wonder why some people want to take credit,
For everything you do.
When they don't make a mark in the field you
Share.
They begin to feel insecure.
As if their loss is somebody's gain for sure.
I wish they didn't underestimate themselves.
They should count their pluses.
Why feel small when others become big in some
Field.
They should take pride in their own achievements.
Dear me,
Belittling others is erroneous,
It does not become you.
Shine at your own steam.
Comparisons don't do well.
You should stay unique.
You are an only woman of your kind.
Live your own life.
Promote and believe in your file.
Leave me alone to shine.
I do, I have been shining and I will.
I have been an achiever,
In quite a few fields.
Since my school days.
No exaggeration.

You are just incidental in my life.
The sooner you believe that,
The better it is for you.
The distance between you and me will grow.
If you continue to act funny.

92

A waft of perfume reached my nostrils
When I sensed you were approaching.
My heartbeat could be heard across the street,
Excitement that I felt was quite a lead.

It was just a chance meeting.
Something about you was appealing.
I could have bet you were special.
Your confidence was unusual.

When our eyes met,
I knew it was a connect.
You would come after me,
You couldn't resist it.

Surprisingly, you didn't.
You must have been jilted.
Once bitten, twice shy.
You would perhaps later try.

We came across each other daily,
He said,' hi ' and smiled drearily.
He didn't even ask my name.
I could discern his pain.

I almost gave up on him.
But soon I was face to face with him.
Strangely though,he excused himself.,
It was over even before I collected myself.

He really was a mystery.
Suspense in the tale was genuine.
Our interaction had been minimal.
He was out of sight for days together.

Why did I begin to miss him?
He wasn't even known to me.
Such attraction is hard to believe.
It affects you but you feel cheated.

It was all a misunderstanding.
He was seen with a woman,
Smiling away to glory.
His girl friend or wife.
Not really shocked,
I just said a quick,' Hi' and' Bye.'

93

Nights are quieter than the day.

The static of TV plays,

Creates enough blare.

All my worries surface then.

Why are my aches and pains,

So prominent at the dead of night.

My fears, my apprehensions are rife.

They attack me in bulk.

I feel restless and anxious.

'Wish life could be better in general

Grass is greener every where else.

Sick of trying to understand everything.

I could try being diplomatic.

Manipulating situations is an art.

You can't always throw darts.

They hurt others as much as they hurt you.

Staying mum makes everything peaceful.

Getting worked up is not good.

It boomerangs on you for sure.

Sleep is always welcome.

The best antidote to every problem.

Get so tired during the day,

Come night and sleep is on its way.

Organise yourself,

Organise your day.

Discipline is required,
To lead a satisfactory life.
If you do not take yourself seriously,
Do not react to any insignificant barb,
Days fly quite simply.

94

Hindu,

Muslim,

Christian,

Parsi,

Indian

Pakistani,

American,

German

All words refer to people living on Earth.

Why then hate one another?

We do need religion to relate to.

But not tolerating somebody's faith is insane.

Making statements derogatory to the country,

Any pricking remark about one's religion,

Leads to distasteful and outrageous reactions.

Moderation and discretion in what you say,

Doesn't hurt any body.

Why can't people hold their tongue?

Why can't they accept the fact,

We are all one,

Colour of the skin,

Your religion,

No doubt might be different.

But your country is supreme.

Why do then our country men, isolate and attack

A particular religion.

Do not say things you know are sensitive.

Terror and intolerance must be fought together.

Loud mouths condemned and punished.

Giving a free reign to such disruptive elements,

Leads to a lot of harm.

Let your country celebrate being different.

There should be unity in diversity.

Being secular doesn't mean,

You can't preserve your heritage,

Our festivals, our ceremonies,

Our architecture, our languages,

Our literature all bespeak of,

Our multifarious expressions.

Our culture is all inclusive.

Don't let one religion be pitted against the other.

Welcome all.

Devote your energies in catching the culprits.

Use intelligence services,

To collect information about terror attacks,

Riots waiting to happen,

Prevent killings of innocent people.

Let all nations get together to fight the scourge of
Terror.

It can be eliminated with strategies devised
Together.

Political shenanigans must be controlled.

Let sanity prevail.

The common man suffers,
If riots happen, individuals attacked,
The party that rules has to ward off the tussle,
Between different religions.
It should be voted out,
If it fails to bring about changes for the better.
Though biased opposition must be rational,
Play a constructive role.
Discuss issues sensibly,
Pass important bills.
Help build the nation.
Offer critical appreciation.
Encourage schemes to help all segments.
Support decisions to build industries, farms,
Roads,
Encourage skill development institutes,
Bank accounts for the poor.
24×7 power and water supply.
Freedom of expression,
But help avoid Hindu, Muslim, Christian vendetta.
And eradicate corruption and disease.
Let trade and e- trade flourish.
Give equal rights to all retailors.
Let quality in goods be controlled.
Honesty and sincerity in dealings be the norm.
Let our country and our country men rise.
Gain prestige for its economic power, progress,
Disciplined people and all inclusive culture.

Let our country men love each other.
Work together, tolerate each other.
Let us build an image we are proud of.
Welcome guests like we love Gods.
You will see happy people.
Contented citizens.
Won't that be great?

95

Mom, I am much older than you now.

I am 67.

You died at 56.

You were a mother of 6 children.

I have had no children.

I know the struggle you went through,

In raising us.

You and dad never let us down.

We were proud of both of you.

Together you built a nest for us.

Gave us comforts and education.

You worked so that we could be brought up,

Without any deprivation.

Every penny you earned was used for our

Upbringing.

The values you taught us,

Have aided us to become responsible citizens.

At my age I still feel you were wiser beyond words.

I have never felt I am more knowledgeable than

You.

Mom, you were an icon.

Being an AIR artist and a school teacher,

You had an aura around your countenance.

Your talent, your sociable nature,

Your immense confidence, your sweet tongue,

Your affectionate and polite demeanour,

Your influence, your connections,

Your actions, your cool temperament.

Your capacity to handle pricky situations

All made you quite a heroine.

You were my idol.

Beyond compare.

I have never come across a woman like you.

I miss you,mom.

I often hurt you with my rigid stands.

Dad loved me no end,

But he loved you so much,

He didn't like me hurting you.

He thought I was responsible for your health

Problems.

I still feel guilty but I had to save myself in time,

To feel okay again.

I wish you could have understood me.

I was happier if not settled exactly.

Well,wishes often jilt us.

We lost you while you were still full of life,

You laughed an open laugh,

Bringing joy to all of us.

Dad was left behind a broken man.

He would never be the same again.

He tried his best to handle us lovingly.

Fulfilling parental duties.

But you left a vacuum.

It could never be filled.

Forgive me for being a cause of your stress.

I would never forgive myself.

I wish you had been more carefree,

We would have had your presence in our lives,

For a few decades more.

Alas, destiny decides when to leave.

I hope wherever you are,

You stay peacefully and happily.

I loved you and dad from the core of my heart.

If I have earned a name for myself,

It is because of the values,

You instilled in me.

The creativity you encouraged in me.

The support you provided all along my life.

I will always be grateful to both of you,

For shaping up my personality,

Giving me immense love and care.

I want to hug you both.

Be with me through my journey in life.

I need your blessings to go on.

I hope you are there somewhere.

Watching your progeny.

You must be proud of each one of them.

They have excelled in their fields.

Credit goes to none other than both of you.

Thank you.

We are what we are because of you.

96

Media helps you reach millions.
Within fraction of a second your statement is
Spread worldwide.
Such accessibility can be both a blessing and a,
Curse.
You just can't retract your words.
Clarification later boomerangs
You are likely to get into trouble.
You can sure promote yourself.
If you endorse some product.
If a well known celebrity says something,
With a shocking value.
It spreads like wild fire.
Whether it was said casually or seriously.
Sometimes it has even international effect.
Therefore caution must be exercised,
Before an icon utters something to the media.
Personal matters don't attract much attention,
But any remark concerned with religion,
Invokes outrageous reactions.
God forbid if some literary figure becomes a victim
Of hate crime,
The media goes on debating its impact on the
Country.
Fellow authors who have been awarded for their

Work,
Begin to return their awards in protest.
Irony of the situation is that,
Religion teaches you to love and be tolerant,
Literature comments on social issues so that,
There is change for the better in the country.
It also just reflects ills and the kind of society,
We live in.
But both are disregarded when it comes to,
Ground reality.
People of different faiths are not congenial with
Each other.
Literary giants forget their duties towards society.
So that only the government has the onus of
Responsibility.
Everything begins and ends with media.
Let media act responsibly.
Let authors divine their responsibility
Let religious heads control the masses.
Let them explain their religious tenets,
To common man.
Understanding between warring factions will
Increase.
Peace will prevail.
Time and energy will be spent on development
Schemes.
Our country will progress.

97

Loves me, loves me not
The game was played when you were in love,
Before you were married.
But after decades of being married,
When your husband seems to have gone astray,
You want to know,
Loves her, loves her not!
It may be just a suspicion.
But such guessing game is played,
Several times in a life time.
A woman won't let her man breathe free.
She becomes obsessive and shrieks,
'Either me or her.'
'Decide.'
Poor man doesn't know how to handle her.
Dinner out or a shopping spree,
Doesn't help much.
Dear men, have your escapades,
But make sure you have an alibi.
A wife's sixth sense smells another woman,
From hundreds of miles!
You can't flaunt the women you conquer.
If you want to save your marriage,
Be diplomatic with your wife.
Come to think of it,

A woman can go astray too.

Better take care,

Let there be love in your relationship,

If you neglect each other.

There is bound to be another person,

Between both of you.

A divorce is not an easy option.

It can turn you into a pauper.

You might even become emotionally disturbed.

Save your marriage by hook or by crook.

Your relationship will be secured for future.

98

When you give me a naughty smile,

I know what's on your mind.

When you hold me tight before you leave me.

I keep yearning for you to come back to me.

Sometimes you click me with your eyes.

As if you have saved me for life.

Why are we always full of apprehensions?

Why don't we stay cool and give up tensions?

It is a mistake to take people for granted.

There is no guaranty your relationship will be

Everlasting.

Like a stone cutter you must work at your

Sculptures.

Real or art structures.

The desire and passion must burn.

To charge up yourself for a longer term.

It is a game you play,

For life and a day.

You can't be a fugitive in your own place.

You get your feet permanently fixed to a spot.

If there is sustainability in your thoughts.

You keep marching ahead to reach your citadel.

Love like everything else changes patterns.

Today it is passion,

Tomorrow it is affection.

Later it is companionship,
A lifelong cosy friendship.
If you love someone,
You are a blessed one.
If somebody loves you,
If he said he did,
If he still does,
You sure are a lucky one.
If love is reciprocal,
Can there be anything more magical?
Freak out often,
Just live it up!
There is nothing more pitiable than a couple,
Who continue to stay together,
But do not love each other.
It is a social commitment,
Nothing more than that.
They also serve who stay together.

99

A shimmering waterfall,
A gracefully gurgling blue water river,
Pure white sheets of snow on mountain peaks,
Trees laden with orange and green autumnal
Leaves,
Fresh snowfall in a hill station,
The vast expanse of chaste waters of the ocean,
A flock of gracefully flying birds,
Rollicking dolphins playfully jumping up in the sea,
A cluster of colourful fish swarming in rivers,
Slowly, languidly swimming ducks in a pond,
The joy of a child learning to crawl on the floor,
Youngsters cycling together on a wide vacant road,
Colourful flowers on flower beds,
Fruit laden trees in an orchard,
The bright stars in the clear blue sky.
What can be more charming than these bites?
Let not the clouds hide your smiles.
Live your life.
Don't drag it laboriously with all your might.
Let there be spring in your steps,
Let there be twinkle in your eyes.
Be energetic to do justice to your life.
Shine like stars.

Dance like colourful flowers.

Keep going peacefully, steadily like a river.

Have depth of the ocean.

Go live life giant size on every occasion.

100

Your mind is split between two sections.
One that is understanding,
The other that thinks of damage to your body and
Soul because of violence and abuse.
Forgiving is not that easy.
You may analyse the source of the problem.
But you suffer the onslaughts on your person.
You can't go out and shout,
'Save me, I am being attacked'
A woman is a very lonely person.
She has to fight her own battles.
Society under plays her case.
She doesn't really have a place.
Parents wash her off their hands,
Once she is married.
Her husband is God who must be worshipped.
Otherwise he will discard their daughter darling,
If she raises her voice against atrocities,
Committed on her.
She is shushed up,
Lest the world knows about it.
The world you hear is changing.
As of now.
When does middle class morality
Vanish, though?

Never, I guess.
Girls will be sacrificed at the alter of marriage.
They will continue to be traumatized and
Demoralized,
Until we wake up to their call of distress.
Women's issues are discussed at forums,
All over the world,
But nothing much changes on the ground.
When do women become spunky enough?
When does the world give a wake up call,
To men in general?
Women shall continue to be second class citizens,
Until they themselves rise to save their kind.
There is no other go.
They will be their own saviours.
Men won't give up being egotistic.
There has to be a revolution to bring about a
Drastic change in their life.

101

How do you structure your time?

Time to wake up.

Time for breakfast.

Time to cook your meals.

Breakfast, lunch and dinner.

Time to write.

Time to read,

The news paper

Or some magazine or a book.

Time to make important calls.

Time to overhaul your ward robe.

Time to attend social dos.

Like weddings and its numerous functions.

Time to rest.

Time to put Refresh tears or Flur in your eyes.

Time to watch TV.

Time to watch DVDs

Time for a walk.

Time for exercise.

Time to take medicine or insulin.

Time to send text messages,

Or emails.

Time to plan shopping trips.

Time to get your Form 16.

Time to file your life certificate.

Time to get caps on your teeth.

Time for eye check ups.

Time to see the Endocrinologist.

Time to sleep.

Time to read Hanuman Chalisa.

Time to do the Healing code.

Time to say Gayatri mantra and other shlokas.

Time to practice singing my favourite songs.

Still whenever I check up Word,

I see 'Welcome back. Pick up where you left off,'

5 hours ago,

3 hours ago,

2 hours ago,

A few seconds ago,

Yesterday

Which only shows,

I have wasted that much time.

Whatever I did during this time was in slow motion.

All the slots I filled could have been done faster to

Save time.

At my age I just do what I must,

And rest of the time,

I am in my bed wrapped up in a blanket,

Thinking of how strange my life is.

Nobody would believe what I go through.

How quietly I count my hours,

How I forgive those who know not what they do,

How I wish to change people around me.

How I write about whatever or whoever touches
Me.
Simple, Mr. Nobody or may be Somebody,
I just use the keyboard.
On my 8 inches tablet.
No Rocket Science, buddy!

102

You see the world of the disabled,

When your mirror shows you are disabled.

As a normal person when you look at somebody,

Who is handicapped,

You just go past him,

Without giving a second glance,

Unless you see a disabled beggar.

You throw a few coins in his hands.

I lost my leg just a few months ago.

Walking with a prosthesis is cumbersome.

Wearing it for a long time is tiresome.

Visits to the clinic off and on are mandatory.

The prosthesis is tweaked or renewed if needed.

What is special about these visits is,

You meet fellow disabled of all ages.

My heart went out to a young woman,

Who had her right leg amputated when she was 12.

Exceptionally good looking at 27,

She had come from abroad.

She was keen to get a prosthesis which looked real.

She wanted to dance at her engagement and

Wedding.

Her looks had attracted a handsome guy.

She was soon getting engaged to that boy.

She naturally wanted to please her beau

She threw tantrums even if it was a little tight or
Loose.
She had to catch her flight back home that day.
Every assistant attended to her almost neglecting
Others.
Nobody minded.
She was being clicked by most of us.
She had come with heavy make up.
She wanted to live in our hearts forever.
I took her pictures with and without her prosthesis.
I was told she had been very generous.
She had brought expensive gifts for the doctors.
She treated every one with chocolates before she
Left.
She was so excited when she got her almost natural
Leg.
She started dancing and took a bow like a performer.
It was so wonderful to see her flash smiles at every
One.
Thank God medical science has invented artificial
Limbs.
Young people like this beauty queen,
Who lost her leg to cancer,
Can live an almost normal life.
As for me I have lived my life.
Losing 1/3rd of my leg at 66,
Was of course shocking and painful.
I am thankful that I didn't lose it when young.

Comparing yourself to those who suffer more,
Makes you feel you haven't suffered that much
Loss.
I keep my morale high.
I think my attitude is right.
I must avoid going into depression.
I do not want to give others a bad impression.
I have been a survivor,
Definitely a fighter.
I will not give up.
I can see a bright future for me.
As long as I can continue to be me.

103

Being punctual is a good habit.

If you are punctual for an appointment,

With your physician,

You should be punctual,

To reach your place of work too.

And meet friends at a fixed time.

Unfortunately,

You are late for everything.

Partly because of traffic jams,

Or just because you got up late,

Or you never thought it was a crime.

Or being a civilian it never registered,

That being punctual is expected.

If you are in the forces,

You dare not report late.

You are likely to be punished.

At weddings only a fool arrives on time.

The groom arrives with his 'procession'

Several hours late.

Only the pundit demands the ceremony

Must begin at the auspicious time designated,

Which is usually past midnight.

If you must have dinner at the wedding,

Don't be surprised if you get it only a little before

Midnight.

We generally don't bother about being punctual.
That's a national weakness,
No wonder nothing gets done on schedule.
Wherever we are we just ignore looking at the
Watch.
Be punctual, stay progressive.
Demand sticking to timings.
You will not regret it.
Leave the place if you are the only one.
Who is on time.
The host will know you came and left.
They will feel guilty for being very late.
Probably they will learn from it.
Arriving late is not something to boast about.
Punctuality is a virtue,
Cultivate it.
You will be a success in life.

104

I want to dance sometimes,
The young girl in me has desires.
They lie buried in me.
You scratch and find me.
I twist and foxtrot,
Shake a leg and move a lot.
I glam up and look hot.
Remember all the compliments I ever got.
I like singing too.
I may not be a professional singer.
But I sing songs with romantic lyrics.
Romance flourishes in flicks with songs.
Real life is not the same as reel life.
You tend to take your family for granted.
Routine kills romance.
You don't feel the need to ignite it.
There are other family issues,
Which demand your time and energy.
Even vacation breaks are not treated as vacation.
Aged parents or grand parents too demand your
Attention.
Romance between a married couple is seldom
Considered important.
Mother's day and Father's day are celebrated.
Something special is done for them.

But have you ever heard of a wife's day or a
Husband's day?
Valentine's day is usually observed by young
Boys or girls.
Anyway singing or dancing cheer your heart.
They are good for your body and soul.
Even if there is no romance,
Even if you don't sing romantic songs,
Even if you don't make romantic dance moves,
But sing and dance for fun or exercise.
It pays you dividends.
You stay physically and mentally healthy.
Do give yourself time.
You need to pamper yourself,
Even if nobody else does.
Live,woman, live.
You deserve a happy life.
It is God's gift.
Value it.
Live it up.
You are the most important person in your life.

105

Whenever you read quotations about love,

You find you don't fit into anyone of them.

Are they really about real people?

Or they refer to something that ought to be.

They are so goody, goody.

Too good to be true.

May be you have yet to understand what love is.

Even after having been in love for a while.

I guess,you will need a next life to find true love,

To get to know the person who will love you.

Or what love is all about.

Is it attraction?

Is it lust?

Is it just staying together?

To live just for the day and feel great.

To do something for your mate?

To put up with negativity in the person?

To not quit though you think you should.

Come just about anything?

To agree even if you don't agree.

To be able to survive onslaughts of every kind?

There are so many questions percolating in your
Mind.

Quotations are often witty.

They give ideas to live life better.

They often inspire you.

They are crisp and pithy.

But they do not tell the whole truth.

They are written out of context.

Therefore,they are half truths.

Or they may express,

What a few individuals may have felt.

They are not universally true.

But they are nice to read at least.

If you copy them,

Try to live them,

You will have a tough time,

For they just talk about wishful thinking.

Real life is more complicated.

I am dead sure about it.

Prove me wrong,

If you can.

Try to get under the skin of the quote.

Don't just forward them to friends on social media,

And feel proud about your belief in the ideas.

Dissect every word.

Draw a conclusion for or against.

I hope to find a lot of people,

Who will vehemently support me.

Quotations on love are well said.

I seldom get to say 'well done' to any one,

Who falls in love.

I wish love couples continue to value,
Loyalty, understanding, sense of fun,
Sharing, desire, passion and caring.
All things positive.
They just disagree.
They don't fight it out.
They just resolve issues peacefully.
They never resort to violence or abuse.
Perhaps they ought to realise,
How lucky they are.
To be really in love.
You know that love is not planned.
It just happens.
Arranged marriages are compromises.
Some lead to love.
Most do not.
Do fall in love.
But do learn the permutations and combinations,
To stay in love.
Love is then a blessing.

106

When you speak,

You communicate.

The way you speak,

Conveys your intention.

You may be taunting.

You may be trying to hurt.

The import your words carry,

Is more important, therefore.

Choose your words carefully.

Weigh your words,

Before you shoot.

Hold your tongue,

When you must.

Very mature people only practice restraint.

Others follow free for all strategy.

Some are not smart enough to have a good

Vocabulary.

They don't make efforts to learn either.

Public Speaking is an altogether different skill.

You have to have confidence to speak.

You maintain the unity of purpose.

You use the right register.

The ease with which you speak,

The knowledge about your subject,

All receive applause from your audience.

If you have the sincerity of purpose.
You are the winner.
Do prepare what you plan to speak on.
It helps you reach your goal.
However life skills should include speech training.
Your mother tongue as well as universally spoken
English,
Need your time and inclination.
They help interact with almost every one.
You get the hang of right words.
You learn to be discreet,
You use caution and refinement in your
Communication.
As you choose your clothes according to the
Situation,
You must choose appropriate words in every
Situation.
Sermonising is easy!
Practicing what you preach is not all that easy.
We must try at least
We must master communication skills.
Develop enough confidence to present
Our case with ease.

107

When young you dare to dream.
Any boy who takes interest in you,
Becomes somebody special.
Your heart begins to beat.
You take more interest in your looks.
You spend a lot of time before the mirror.
You spread your wings like a butterfly.
Your steps show your impatience.
Your interest in music is back in full swing.
Romantic numbers catch your attention.
You begin to mumble the songs.
They convey your state of mind.
The joy dies down as the man shifts to another
Town.
Such encounters happen few and far between.
Once you catch the match,
You get married,
Life changes quite a bit.
You are introduced to family.
By and by the bride is taken over by a housewife.
The equation with your mate changes.
Your only task is to keep the family together.
Life goes on.

The flame of love is gradually extinguished.

You are just a robot.

Going through the routine like a machine.

Romance is found in fiction.

Real life is monotonous, you know the reason.

You carry on with your familial and social duties.

You try to keep every one happy.

You often take up a placement,

To balance the family budget.

You are glorified as a woman of substance.

It does help in your sustenance.

108

The crescent moon shining in the dead of night.
Brings good tidings from afar.
Reassuringly looks at you.
It burns bright'
All the night.
Even though it is not the full moon,'
It is still quite a boon,
It peeps through the sky.
It is strategically placed giving us light.
O,my fellow resident of the universe!
Your beautiful look fascinates us.
Don't ever disappear from the nightly panorama
The Earth needs you to stay put wherever you are.
There is nothing in the universe,
As attractive as you.
You are the Muse of poets.
A subject for astronomers,
Geographically interesting.
Cool and soothing.
An inspiring presence.

· 109 ·

The gleam in your eyes,
Indicated your confidence in your profile.
Having studied at a prestigious university,
You bagged a couple of degrees.
Hunted for suitable placements.
You found your life's vocation.
You fancied yourself quite a catch.
In the marriage market.
But life turned upside down,
When you blindly accepted a marriage proposal,
At the behest of your family.
Trusting them to choose the best for you.

The first encounter with the man at the wedding,
Shocked you out of your senses.
You wanted to get up from the altar.
To run away from the scene,
As the groom looked very old,
And was very crude and rough in his ways.
You felt betrayed by your family.
But you didn't have the courage to defy them then.
It was your fault.
Why didn't you see him before the wedding?
It was perhaps too late to quit.
After having interacted with him a couple of times,

And finding nothing as a saving grace,
You made up your mind to leave him.
And save your life.
It was next to impossible to dream of life with him.
He didn't have anything you could have liked.
As soon as you had a chance to speak with him.
You told him in no uncertain terms that you wanted
To go back home.
Luckily for you nothing physical had happened
Between you and him.
The marriage was not consummated either.
The break up was going to be clean.
Eventually, you convinced your folks that,
It was a mismatch.
You had expected better judgement on their part.
You wasted seven golden years of your youth,
To get an annulment of the marriage legally.
Once free of the bond.
You were pressurised to marry again.
After a few years you did find a match.
That is another story.
Wait, if you want to catch it.
Life for some is never easy.
It teaches you quite a few lessons.
Know the truth.
Destiny decides a lot for every one of you.
However, you can build your life on certain,
Positives in your married status.

Which keep nourishing you for life.
Keep your future secure for all time.
You count your blessings and carry on.
Society gives you a thumbs up.
It certainly keeps your morale up.

110

The eternal question you ask yourself is,
What to cook for lunch or dinner?
You make separate breakfast for every one,
As the choice differs from person to person.
Some want bread and eggs, some porridge,
Some rolled and fried Indian parantha or roti.
Lunch is usually typically Indian.
Veggies, pulses and curds with 'chapattis'.
Which vegetable or which 'dal',you are in a fix.
Using your discretion you choose what fits in.
Five to six o'clock rings in tea time.
Normally biscuits and light snacks are fine.
Dinner is a fancy meal.
You have to make it a treat.
As every member of the house is at the dining
Table.
You choose the menu out of several cuisines,
You go to You Tube to dig out unique recipes.
A woman feels inadequate if she doesn't cook
Trendy, delectable meals.
Chinese,Mexican,Japanese or Continental.
Her repertoire is full if she learns soups, non-veg,
Or vegetarian specials like Murg Mussalam or Gobhi
Mussalam, Biryani or Quiche, pies cakes or cookies.
If you are a good cook you go through short courses

On how to make,sauces,pickles and squashes.
Half a woman's life is spent being in the kitchen.
But the compliments she receives are priceless.
Scrumptious, sumptuous,luscious and tasty !
All these adjectives make your day.
It makes you feel loved and wanted everyday.
Food is a great connector,
The family members remain linked with each other.
They exchange the day's news at the dining table.
The housewife is the catalyst who brings them
Together.
Long live the housewife who is always ready to
Cook delicious meals for her family and friends.

111

Juvenile bill was finally given a green signal.
Never ever believed fledglings could be criminals.
Twenty first century's kids are techno savvy.
A three year old is seen taking a selfie.
A little older kid freely uses the mobile.
Children of all ages have become quite volatile.
Tablets and IPads are used for gaming activities.
The games teach violence and speeding but keep
Them busy.
Instead of learning life skills they seek pleasure.
Pornography is available on the click of a button.
Their innocence is lost once they get inducted into
Kinky sex and drugs.
Rapes and molestation cases multiply,
Quite a few of them are committed by juveniles.
So far juvenile delinquents up to the age of 18 years
Were sent to remand homes for three years.
They were not punished like adults.
After the brave heart got brutally gang raped,
The juvenile who committed the heinous crime,
Along with some adults, was released after three
Years.
All right minded people were outraged
The parents staged a protest demanding death
Penalty for the juvenile rapist too.

Hundreds of people supported them.

Justice was denied to the Braveheart.

She had lost her life after the brutal rape.

The anger that brewed after her death,

Resulted into candle light vigils and demand for

Adequate penalty for the rapists.

A demand to change the law,which left juveniles

Go scot-free after three years, was made.

It wasn't taken up while the juvenile was under

Care of the government.

The moment it was decided to release him,

A volcano erupted.

How could a juvenile commit such a crime !

Perhaps his age in records wasn't entered right.

Whatever,there was a cry to bring down the age

From 18 to 16 to punish children who commit,

Serious crimes such as murder or rape.

Thankfully the parliament passed this bill.

The brave heart may not have got justice.

But it would be a deterrent for the young to get

Involved in crimes.

Parents would also be warned to teach the right

Values to their children.

Well ! Time will only tell how it changes the mind

Set of the citizens of this country.

We hope every woman is given security on roads,

Lanes and by lanes.

She should fearlessly be able to travel in public

Transport.
She should get education in healthy environment.
Boys and men must learn to help women,
Instead of victimising them.
We can only hope and pray for this miracle.
Talking about reforms or security is easy.
Ground reality will not change in a jiffy.
Efforts must continue to provide safety for women.
Then only these terrified women will feel safer.
Isn't that a comment on our sick society?
Women not only suffer violence and abuse at
Home,
They are raped,trafficked and trivialised,
Sexually harassed and get biased treatment,
At work.
When do we expect to get equal treatment?
When do we feel strong and independent?
We do face challenges as women,
But we still often rue being women.
How long?
God only knows!

112

Mathematics is a dragon feared by most students.
They can never figure out what is odd and what is
Even.
What is an equation or what is a theorem.
They keep Algebra, Geometry, Arithmetic and
Statistic a pole's length away.
They like to indulge in speed driving,
Just for a kick.
Drink,drug and dames,
Three D's are game.
They now are forced to learn their basic math.
Pollution Level in their town have become
Dangerous.
The CM wants odd number cars,
And Even numbers cars,
To ply on alternate days.
Women,VIPs, ambulances,autos and fire tenders,
However are allowed on all days.
But I am worried about all those who will forget
If it is odd or even number day.
They have never been good at Math anyway!
Their conclusions will be fudged because they have no
presence of mind.
Their confusion will result in disobeying the law.
They will have to pay a huge fine.

The side effect of the law will be,
Otherwise law abiding citizens will learn to cheat.
If they have a car with an odd number license
Plate,
They will buy one with an even number license
Plate.
The more the cars the more pollution.
If there is no strict check on numbers,
Some might hood wink the cops on duty.
With so many exemptions I am not sure it is going
To work.
Anyway at least the government realises,
The pollution levels are dangerously high in the
Town.
They will go on trying other alternatives,
To fight the monster of pollution.

–

113

As a young girl I had lovely long tresses.
I would blush whenever somebody complimented
Me.
At home I always left them open.
I was criticized for not being modern.
It wasn't really chic.
When today I see girls with elaborate fringes,
And long hair.
I feel jealous!
I used to love keeping them open!
If my fiancé hadn't ordered me to trim them,
I would never have shortened them.
I loved my hair to distraction.
My friends wanted to see me married.
As I had not ever said 'yes' to any body.
They too advised me not to displease him.
I used to wonder why I must do what he wanted.
I should go in for what I liked.
A colleague just dragged me to her room one day,
She took out a pair of scissors and forcibly cut
The length of my hair.
I looked bewildered but I let it happen.
Secretly I also didn't wish to annoy him.
If I couldn't do it, at least somebody else did it

For me.

Once my hair had a cut,

It was easier to get a shorter cut.

The next few days I went to work with my head

Covered.

I felt so self conscious and shy,

As I didn't like my new style.

I missed my long hair which I could set

To any which way I would select.

It was like losing my best asset.

It is more than 30 years now,

I still long for those tresses falling down.

My long plait, my bun, my chignon.

My bangs,my pony tails,my knotted braid.

They used to get me lots of compliments.

Later I tried to grow them to a fashionable length.

I couldn't manage that feat.

Finally,I gave up chasing the impossible dream.

I got adjusted to the short boyish cut.

I often regret having got them cut.

To gain something, must you lose something?

Your husband needn't be the lord of the ring.

Poor me !

My poor parents!

They wanted to see me wear a ring!

All to get me married.

How long girls will continue to sacrifice their choices at

The altar of marriage?

You definitely make adjustments with your new family
And your dear husband.
But at least you should be allowed to be yourself.

114

Carcinogenic chemicals,
The incoming trucks,
Neck to neck traffic,
Building materials.
Burning garbage,
Diesel vehicles,
Burning dry leaves,
Winter fires
All cause polluted air.
Danger to life.
Don't waste time.
Think fast.
How to save ourselves from this crime?
Odd number,
Even number cars,
Match them to,
Odd days,
Even days drive.
Let us see how they fare,
How they purify the air.

· 115 ·

We stood under the lemon tree,

The yellow lemons,raw lemons,

Why do lemons look tempting hung on trees?

Think about it.

Lemons used in dressings enhance the taste.

Don't they?

Life has been juicy but often sour too.

As in grapes are sour!

But we are still together.

Looking up the lemon tree.

Hoping for lemons to fall.

As if they are gold.

Stupid us!

Life might become a bit spicy if we get some!

It is so adventurous to pluck them.

Reach them with a bamboo.

And get a big haul of them.

Shopping for them is so crass.

So inane.

Routine is so tiresome.

How to break the monotony?

Make the most of your lemon tree!

Future seems so blank.

Nothing to look forward to.

Each day that we confront.

Yields nothing but breaths.
Should you begin to count them?
Count down seems to have begun.
But you cannot ever be sure.
How and when life ceases to be.
You must identify the sore points.
Try every remedy that works on them.
A miracle might happen.
To bring you back to life again.
Dying is as difficult as life.
They are two sides of the same coin.
Live while you can.
Even if plucking random stuff from a tree.
Death is for sure.
Just as you don't recall your birth.
You won't know that you are dead.
The two ends cover a sentence.
A SENTENCE. Got it?
The beginning and the full stop.

116

Words seek to fly,
The sky is clear.
Yet they fail to take off.
They must be uttered.
Something in you hesitates to do so.
The heart is not ready to give in.
What if they meet the dead end?
Why invite embarrassment?
If the future is going to be yours,
It will be yours.
Let him throw his weight around.
Just stick to your ground.
Stability is worth achieving.
It points to your upbringing.

117

I exist.

You exist.

If we exist together,

We resent each other.

Space is necessary between people.

Walls give you shelter.

They protect you from going helter skelter.

They give you opportunities to think and plan.

Unfortunately,despite all facilities,

We fail to understand each other.

'Suspension of disbelief.'

'Stream of consciousness.'

'Existentialism.'

All contribute to our confusion.

Life has no logic.

Half the things people say are not intended.

You try to be rational.

Still words often mislead you.

Overlapping of thoughts and emotions

Is a regular phenomenon.

Yet we are ready to try out new ideologies.

New challenges.

Push,

Assert yourself.

Speak up.

Shout,if not heard.

Slam unfair criticism.

Shun troublesome people.

Read realistic stories.

The lessons learnt help in your development.

Debate ideas to be implemented.

Be loyal.

Be patriotic.

Love your fellow human beings.

Love yourself.

Extend your reach.

Don't just exist.

Live!

Handle,

Whatever destiny throws at you.

118

She was a beautiful young girl.
Looking into the mirror was her love.
Even if a pimple was noticed,
She felt agitated.
If any strand of her hair turned prematurely grey,
She would raise a hue and cry and pray,
"Please God don't punish me."
"I wouldn't want to face anybody,
If I begin to look old in my prime.
That is something I wouldn't like."
She continued to be jazzy.
She stood out in a group of beauties.
Fate had something else in store.
She wanted to be a working woman, nothing more.
Having finished her education,
She was employed as a teacher.
She was lucky to fulfil her mission.
She had achieved her ambition.
She used to walk down to her school.
A young man often followed her route,
He made a pass at her quite often.
She wanted to share her concern.
She informed her family about it.
Her father promised to tackle it.
He didn't want to go to the police.

So he decided to get her married.

That man on the street came to know about it.

One fine day he accosted her.

He was daring enough to say he loved her.

She was a dream girl for him.

He would like to meet her family.

But she began to feel uneasy.

Her family wouldn't welcome just anybody.

She told him to back off.

She didn't like road side Romeos.

Still he persisted.

Followed her everywhere.

She again spurned him rudely.

One day while she was leaving school.

He threw acid on her face.

She cried,"Save me,"

But nobody came forward to help.

They perhaps feared,

They would be attacked too.

She was later hospitalised

Her skin on the face was burnt.

She couldn't have looked into the mirror.

Her dreams were shattered.

Slowly and steadily she recovered.

But her beautiful looks were distorted.

She would never be married.

Her family felt helpless.

Surgeries after surgeries,

Her face had become a patch work.

Nothing less or nothing much.

Alas ! We fail to teach our sons,

That they should respect women.

They are into eve teasing.

They are into gang raping.

They are into other crimes.

They have not been trained to live clean life.

They are into domestic violence.

Women should not remain silent.

They must learn to raise their voice.

They have no other choice.

If only young men had suitable employment.

If they could make good decisions.

If their families were tolerant

They would be civilized men.

Women would feel safer.

Life for everybody will be happier.

· 119 ·

What if she runs away?

Where would she go?

Relatives might welcome her for a few days.

She could live alone, perhaps.

She might breathe fully.

But soon money crunch would hurt.

No gainful work will be given to her.

She is too old to work.

She is a handicapped person.

She might wrench out alimony.

They might divide their assets.

Everything takes time.

Surviving alone will be a battle.

Sooner or later she'll break.

Getting old is so frustrating.

You are retired.

Your body is weak.

You need to be looked after.

But if you have no children.

If your partner wants his way always.

You remain tense.

There is no scope for discussion.

Your will is superfluous.

It doesn't work out.
It doesn't work out.
Stuck for life.
Is she?

120

When I am unwell,

I want to be left to myself.

I just need to cuddle into bed.

May be want a cup of tea.

More than that,

I need to talk on the mobile to somebody.

Exchanging news with a friend,

Expels all silly thoughts from your head.

Enquiring about her health,

Or about her daily tussles,

Diverts your mind from your own troubles.

Friends do play an important role.

They try to analyse what's wrong,

Give you valuable advice.

You begin to feel nice.

The sequence of turning points in your life,

Do have riders.

You take big risks.

Yet nothing is always hunky dory.

You fight it out,

This is how you survive.

Women are more resilient.

Men are egotistic, rigid but have more strength.

The struggle between them,

Will continue to go on,hence.

Somethings never change.

You have to be trained.

Otherwise you badly fail.

Parents pamper you no end.

A husband takes your hand,

Lands you from heaven to Earth.

If your grip on life is strong.

You will survive despite everything being wrong.

But it is no life you dreamt of.

The sky was the limit.

Your smile was more than a mile.

You flew looking for a prize.

Your bright eyes,

Your wings so wide.

Your ambition so high.

Your hopes visualised in terms of delight.

All crashed once you were attached.

Alas, it is real life.

No romantic cinema.

Songs and dialogues.

Hugs and kisses.

Dates and bike rides.

The End,

When happily united.

Actually that is the beginning!

All hell breaks loose!

Road to heaven is lost!

You are lost!

Take a lift.

No way.

Your life is one track.

Stay there.

Middle class woman,

Nobody can help you.

Continue to drag your life.

You deserve it.

You are a coward!

You sermonise but you can't manage your life.

You want to end up in suicide?

Never. Never. Never.

Carry on then.

Lets see how it ends.

121

How shall I put it?

You brought some sweetness into my life.

Even though temporarily.

It was fun while it lasted.

I used to feel my life had no bright spots.

I was wrong.

Even though the moments had a short span,

It restored my confidence back.

Was I lucky?

We are responsible if we invest more in something

Fragile.

We must stop being greedy if life shines on us just

For a while.

As the nature of things go,

Day and night are real, we know.

Why then raise your expectations?

Enjoy the sunshine.

Sleep the night.

Days will go by.

Leaving memories.

They will give you sustenance.

For periods of disturbance.

122

Reading news paper is a habit.

TV reports stretch news quite a bit.

The panel debates raise your blood pressure.

Often the same speakers are booked for several
Channels.

It is unsettling to hear over and over again the same
Individuals.

Very seldom they get to command full attention.

News papers any day are a better option.

You read quietly as if you are in meditation.

Although news covers city events, accidents,

Political developments, International matters.

Even if you just read headlines,

You get the import of the underlines.

TV anchors adopt a condescending attitude.

Nobody in the panel gets enough latitude.

Still the panellists take it easy.

They don't give up though they visibly feel uneasy.

The debate ends in half cooked wind ups.

There are 100 to 115 Breaking News headlines on
Some channel.

They sensationalise almost every news which is at
Best topical.

Your heartbeat goes faster as they illustrate each
News.

Headlines in the news papers have dual meaning.
Often there are interesting puns.
It becomes a game to identify the most complicated
Ones which is fun.
At a certain age you look for peaceful stuff.
So news papers give you the liberty to choose,
What you love.
You turn to sports or cultural events, comics,
Puzzles or Sudoku.
Violence,political shenanigans,accidents,
Update the negatives in society,
You can just glance through them,
Unless they teach you important lessons.
As for me I'll pick up a news paper any day.
TV news gives you migraine practically every day.
Switch off couch potatoes your 40 inches or
Something TV sets.
Instead go for a morning walk,take a news paper
Along.
After a strenuous walk,relax on a bench,
Read what you fancy in the news paper to your
Heart's content.
Fresh in the body,fresh in the mind,
You certainly feel sublime!
Two hoots,
To TV news!
Hip, Hip hurray,
To news papers!

123

Life can give you shocks.
A person who is into regular walks,
Exercise regimen, diet control,
Is expected to stay healthy for long.
A close relative with such habits,
Is hospitalized for by pass surgery.
She is of course a diabetic,
She is on insulin.
Is Diabetes the culprit?
She is only 69.
Is age playing volatile?
May be she indulges herself.
Takes artificial sugar products.
She probably thinks they are harmless.
We have to go to the depth of the matter.
The products sold for diabetics are to blame.
They are actually harmful.
Consumers are fooled.
They blissfully believe they are sugar free.
They are full of calories.
Ignorant victims begin to over eat.
They think they can enjoy a treat.
Most people have a sweet tooth.
Why should they shun something good?.
They go ahead and indulge.

They satisfy their urge.

Traders would do anything to sell their products.

We just cannot trust.

Dear misguided health conscious people,

Please before you buy eatables look at the label.

My protagonist is due for surgery anytime.

We wish her a very long and healthy life.

124

Why do we want to have a long life?

Because we generally feel fine.

In moments of frustration,

We want to cut short our breaths.

As there is a dark tunnel ahead.

No exit is visible from a distance.

When you can't see a way out,

You think of suicide day in and day out.

Brave people go on suffering,

Hoping for some positive changes.

It is a dicey situation.

You just wait for destiny's decision.

You wish to confide in someone,

Most people remain formal while talking.

They cannot be trusted with confidential things.

When you wash your dirty linen in public.

It makes matters complicated.

There is no option but to stoically stay put.

Accept your lot with fortitude.

Some day some miracle might happen,

With a magic wand your life may become better.

If not,seek advice.

There are people who are exceptionally nice.

Counsellors can also provide aid.

It is your birth right to get love not hate.

There is nothing that you lack.

Your looks are presentable enough.

You are,without doubt, intelligent.

You are financially sound.

You have a good reputation around.

You had a brilliant career.

You do everything a woman is expected to do.

Why then go on putting up with an idiotic fool?

Why not put up a fight?

Why not do something right?

Confront the perpetrator.

Bring him to confess his unpardonable behaviour.

Your boldness might change ground reality.

Otherwise you will remain an object of pity.

You have the option.

Use it.

Don't cry.

Try.

The cool and courageous,

The gutsy and gracious,

Win the battle.

We wish you well!

125

When you put your arms around me,
And whisper sweet nothings in my ears
The world suddenly looks sweeter.
Words become superfluous,
Silent connect speaks for us.

Suddenly I fly all over,
Wanting not to stop anywhere.
Wait for you to look up.
Gauging the thoughts I do not utter.

I,sure. am not me.
I go through a metamorphosis.
Suddenly I want to look at my best.
I go on humming romantic ballads.

I just can't look into your eyes.
They tell me come closer,don't feel shy.
Hugs and kisses follow.
It feels hot.
You need time to cool off.

Loving some one is not funny.
Longing for someone is agony.
If you part for some reason.

The pangs of love haunt you forever.

Stay true in love till you die.
Ups and downs,smiles and frowns.
Will make a part of your life.
You will be together for miles.

126

These days private hospitals are like five star
Hotels.
Very clean,sanitized,air-conditioned,
Super toilets for Men and Women.
Organised waiting rooms with sufficient
Chairs.
Elevators, Enquiry desk, Booking counters, and
Chemists.
Ventilated corridors,, parking lots, and canteens.
They maintain quality in architecture.
Whether it be OPD, OT, ICU or kitchen.
Doctors are seen going up and down in their,
Surgical outfits usually in sky blue colour.
There are cubicles with stylish furniture,
The specialists have them for consultations,
With their patients.
Well, the hospital is worth a walk.
Being an indoor patient is nothing short of being a
Star.
You are in ICU for a heart ailment.
Nurses try everything to make you comfortable.
Once you are shifted to CCU.
A team of doctors flock around you.
They whisper observations and opinions
About your condition.

After angiography and a couple of stents,
You are shifted back to your ward.
Next day after you are out of sedation,
They shift you to your own single room.
Everything seems to go fine.
They prepare a discharge slip.
Soon they give you a list of your medicines.
You go through discharge routine.
Your family pay up the dues.
With discharge report you come back home.
Nothing substandard, all told.
You feel better.
You know your life is extended.
A fortune was paid for this period.
In some cases insurance cover is given.
And you don't feel the money crunch.
But God save you if you have to bear the brunt.
There is a big hole in your pocket.
After all you had five star comforts and treatment.
Civil hospitals cater to either poor or middle class
Patients or politicians who have exclusive wards,
And get special attention.
A general walk through these hospitals shows you
Poor sanitation,space crunch, shortage of beds,
Crowded corridors and urine stench.
Why this negligence for the state hospitals?
Why this disparity?
The common man goes on suffering on other fronts

Too.

Political parties just wait for elections.

They want important positions in the seat of
Power,

So that they can give speeches and fool the
Innocent citizens.

Wake up my fellow countrymen.

Work towards a better nation.

Vote carefully.

Demand standards.

Don't let them enjoy their fat pay packets.

Country's resources must be yours to share.

127

Come winter,
You love to be in bed under cover.
You curl like a baby and make crazy sounds.
You want to have hot coffee with fritters.
Being pampered feels much better.
Winter has its own charms.
There are so many things to keep you warm.
Indigenous sweets made with jaggery and sesame
Seeds, peanuts,walnuts,cashewnuts and raisins.
A glass of wine, brandy or champagne is divine.
But close hugs with your loved ones are extra nice.
Your warm inners, jackets,pull overs with mufflers,
All branded and fashionable, make you look special.
You keep getting compliments from every one.
It is a pleasure to soak in sunshine in the balcony,
Munching goodies especially hot snacks with
Chutney.
Relaxing in cosy armchairs with friends and family,
Chatting nineteen to a dozen with Tom, Dick and
Harry.
Working people sit out in lawns of their office
Complex.
They play cards and share their lunch packs with friends.
Cricket commentary, FM radio with film songs,
Provide good entertainment while you go for a

Stroll.

A family sitting together in the Sun clicks a good
Selfie in winter

The chill of minus tempratures,foggy weather,
Make you shiver.

Though brief, winter break brings a lot of cheer.

Children go outside to play with their peers

Sultry weather in summer makes you irritable.

Winter spells warmth and makes you feel
Comfortable.

Days go by without any major stress.

Days and nights tell you in plain words.

Life is beautiful and fun.

Winter makes you feel more energetic.

Going out dressed cosily is fantastic.

Some people wait for snowfall in winter.

They rush to the hills to witness white miracle.

There are those who hide in quilts,

They hate the biting chill.

Summery days agree with them.

They keep away their cold related sickness.

Winter any day is better for health.

Your cheeks look bright and red.

All because you enjoy the sunshine and eat well.

Winter goodies do wonders with your health.

Pray for rains in winter.

Nothing could be as full of wonder.

They bring bounty for the farmers.

Winter though short remains a charmer.

128

Chill.

Indulge.

Freak out.

Dance a belly dance.

Sing on karaoke.

Learn Salsa.

Record a song.

Jump on the bed.

Call a wrong number.

Cook Okonomiyaki.

Buy skates.

Stay on fruits for a day.

Chuck laziness.

Go to a mall to enjoy an ice cream bar.

Place an order for pricey jewellery.

Say no to phone calls for a day.

Ask for Virgin Mary as a guest.

Instead if they bring Bloody Mary take it.

Go see a concert.

See the latest movie.

Enjoy popcorns.

Throw a sixer with a ball !

Watch TV's back to back serials for fun.

Don't you cry and run away!

If you wait for someone to give you company,

You will never get to do anything interesting.
Motivation comes from within.
Just make your will power strong.
You will never go in for anything that's wrong.
It is a good idea to make a To do list.
Like I must see the science museum.
I have to buy myself something special,
Especially to celebrate my birthday this month!
Go for a heritage walk with my friends.
Visit Red Cross to donate blankets for the homeless.
Plan to see exhibitions of art, handicrafts,
Handloom and silk fabrics at Dilli Haat.
There are 100 and 1 wonders in your country.
Get set and plan your trips with friendly company.
Never regret that you couldn't live life to make
Yourself happy.
Choose to be happy.
By hook or by crook.
Go have a blast.
Don't hide in a nook,
A lonely bird doesn't last.
Dance and sing like a lark!

129

Home safari?
Yes,home safari.
Sometimes your family members are more
Ferocious than animals.
You let them loose in the house.
Letting them pounce on you.
You expose yourself to danger.
In a moment of madness they try to strangle you.
You have been slapped hard on both your cheeks
With giant hands,
Kicked hard on the chest and abdomen and,
Abused in dirtiest language.
Although you suffer damage to your body.
Life is quieter for a while until the next similar
Episode.
You keep hopping from room to room,
Much like a ride in a vehicle in a jungle safari.
You do view these creatures in a calmer state.
But when there is even a negligible stimulus,
They revert to their basic instincts.
The reaction is disproportionate to the stimulus.
Things normal people handle without trouble,
Are enlarged many times over for these persons.
Sometimes when you come across such men,

You analyse their behaviour pattern,
You do hit the nail on the head.
You conclude that the violent and abusive individual
Suffers from something which is in his genes.
He can perhaps overcome his symptoms if he takes
Help from psychiatrists to understand himself.
But the problem is not all that simple.
Nobody is ready to admit that they have a problem.
They go on torturing their loved ones.
It is sheer luck that nobody reports this case of
Domestic violence to the authorities.
They have escaped punishment so far.
Thus,endangering lives of other family members.
How long such scenario will go on recurring?
When does the jungle turn into a safe home?
When does the round of home safari end?
When do the affected people lead a normal life?
Perhaps never.
Nobody will overcome the phobia of mental
Treatment?
Nothing positive seems to be happening soon.
Every thing for the outsiders is fine.
Such persons have a double mask,
One for the outsiders one for family members.
They feel free to bash up and abuse their close
Relatives.
If only society gets to view the real nature of such
Persons,

They will voice their protest against their,
Behaviour.
Until then,
Keep year fingers crossed.
Nothing untoward happens in your house.
Although butchered to pulp you still remain alive.
Continue to assert yourself and try to do what you
Like.
You remain under constant terror.
It affects the quality of your life.

130

I never knew I could still cry,
Having seen a tragic movie,
I was moved to tears.
Crying is emotionally cathartic.
With tears your body is cleansed.
You feel lighter.
Your feeling that you are strong dissipates.
You are vulnerable like everybody else.
Crying with copious tears twice in a day,
Is nothing short of a miracle.
Interestingly you don't cry on being injured,
But you begin to cry when shown sympathy,
Or your mind and heart are hurt.
Your eyes do not remain dry when you cry.
They wash off all the grit from your eyes.
Tears are something very natural.
Glycerine tears are obviously drama.
They cry this way on screen.
But we think that they are real tears.
We respond to the situation and cry.
You can't cry on command.
Sometimes you are too shocked to cry.
Tears well up in your eyes,
If any emotion touches your heart,
Love too at times wets your eyes.

Just the thought of separation makes you cry.

It just feels lighter to cry for a while.

You reconcile yourself to the situation,

That steals your smiles.

Don't be ashamed of crying.

It is very natural to express your emotions.

Men don't cry is a myth.

When young,their mothers drill it in their minds

That boys are stronger.

Emotionally men are weaker.

They are even less tolerant than women.

Crying helps in certain situations.

Whether you are a man or a woman.

Crying in secret saves you from embarrassment.

131

You have quite a figure.

It is an asset.

You begin to get compliments.

Evil eyes also look at you.

Being a woman is tough.

You are bold and beautiful.

You make a career,

Work, earn and get married.

Yet your daily news folder,

Shows innumerable rapes, murders, suicides,

Dowry deaths, divorces of page 3 socialites or

Famous actors.

'Crimes against women' graph keeps going up.

Why is it a man oriented world?

Why are women tortured?

Why do they have to secretly dump foetuses in

Dustbins?

Why do they jump to death?

Why are they virtually treated as slaves?

Why is the girl child aborted?

Why can't a woman be safe out at

Night?

Why are they made to feel inferior?

A woman is tender, loving and self sacrificing.

Emotionally stronger than men.

Why is she thrown into an unequal world?

Save womanhood God,

If the world wants to save itself.

There is no other go.

Be warned so called omnipotent but foolish men.

Save women from men.

Let them live gracefully

Give them as much love as you can

They will continue to be faithful.

Try it.

Giving is getting.

Know that.

That is the answer to man-woman relationship.

132

Your silence in response to a situation.

Sometimes saves the situation.

You maintain your equilibrium.

You wait for the storm to pass.

You cannot always assess the loss.

Somewhere it leaves destruction.

Of faith,

Of trust,

Of a relationship.

Of upside down strategies.

Of respect,

Of common behaviour.

Of time,

Of wasted energies,

Of the human mind.

A third party can never understand the issue.

Handle on your own.

It is your funeral.

Be there to see yourself dead or die, dive or surface,

Or stay as it is.

No kidding.

Loss occurs if you choose silence.

Loss occurs double fold if you choose to spill the
Beans.

Save yourself.

Nobody can do that.

Specially if you are old enough to handle.

Face it alone.

Go alone.

Be strong.

133

You are as you see yourself in the mirror.
Your age keeps changing every moment.
Anti wrinkle creams notwithstanding.
Your smiles put your wrinkles in the right order.
Your frowns change the shape of your beautiful
Brows.
Your pouts devour your lips.
Especially when your lipstick is on.
Your eyes often reflect the state of your mind.
They twinkle.
They droop with hurt.
They shine with your victories.
They search for quality.
Your ears catch the nuances of comments.
Sweetness of sad songs.
Understatements of jokes.
Your eyes hunt for content,
What you choose to glance at.
The countenance often betrays your heart,
Thus giving people a chance to figure out your
Emotions and thoughts.
Your tears are always confidential.
You don't want to share them with anyone.
Your grim look is acquired with attitude.
Your tense moments also add to it.

Why have a permanent grouse on your face?
Nobody wants you close if you throw your weight
Around.
Why not merge instead of being nerdy?
'Love all, ' says a little birdie.

134

Your window to the world opens,
When you interact with know-all individuals.
It humbles you.
Thanks to them you gain information.
Unfortunately they are not Search Engines.
You can't demand to get information from them.
They connect with you when free from their
Schedule.
It is tiring to log on to relevant topics.
The choices sometimes don't give you exact
Information.
There are no ready made recipes.
Labour is needed for every task.
There are connected links.
There is no dearth of information.
There is knowledge overload.
I wonder by the time those who are children now
Grow up,
They will have no way out of technology.
They will be steeped into it thoroughly.
Poor kids!
Libraries are so much fun.
Interesting titles with colourful covers.
Attract you with the synopses.
You pick up a book for its cover at first glance.

The title announces the content.
You walk past the shelves,
Even discuss in undertones with your pal where to
Go for coffee.
The aisles give you privacy enough to exchange
Glances.
Surely better than Smses!
Two in one task, isn't it?
O, for the romance of it all !
When you were young,
Tutors invited you for tutorials in a nearby coffee
House.
A perfect example of fun and work,they found.
Search of knowledge took you to hills for a trek.
A sheer adventure.
It can't be compared to working on a computer.
An amalgamation of methods should yield better
Results.
You gain knowledge and it is refreshing,yes.
Do tap other resources to update your GK.
Do not spend hours on the internet to get updates,
Unless you are writing a thesis.
You will save your self from spondylitis.

· 135 ·

20 minutes and she will be 68.

Days turn into months,Years into fate.

You can touch the palpable time frames.

Time jumps to reach memorable days.

As a young girl she flew around like a dove.

Overcoming hurdles, dreaming of stars above.

16th year brought college.

An opportunity to gain knowledge.

But it taught several other things on the run.

She delved into logic,ethics,aesthetics,psychology

And Literature.

Experienced intricacies of intimate friendships.

It brought maturity and the power to forgive.

Co-ed education introduced boys in her life.

But her aim was to get a degree or two after a

While.

Employment followed education.

Marriage was on the cards too.

It happened without consent.

Within a few days it saw the end.

A long gap was filled with a job.

Dark night was followed by dawn.

Life turned a little exciting.

As her mate with a new face was seen walking in.

A drastic change definitely.

It continued a little strangely.

Years dragged them as if by violence.

From a girl she flowered into a sensible woman.

A checkered career followed,

Punctuated with something hollow.

Facing twisted,freakish events,

Life turned strife ridden and tempestuous.

She grew stronger and resilient.

One thing she sure has learnt.

You run into unpredictable turns.

Both nice and not so nice ones.

The final curtain call is awaited.

What it brings can't be anticipated.

Old age brings its own problems.

She wishes and hopes that she has no tensions.

Birthday wishes have begun to pour in already

She is ready to see them turn into reality.

She is thankful to her near and dear ones.

She is lucky to have all of them who show concern.

136

Some houses are haunted.

In unsuspecting spaces you feel unwanted.

Discontent grips you now and then.

You get negative vibes.

You just don't feel right.

You often feel unwell.

You sure have bad spells.

You know why?

You can't even share on the sly.

If you want peace in the house.

You have to squeak like a mouse.

Just stand at attention.

Give salute of 32 guns.

If you wish to last in your home.

Otherwise you will end up in a tomb.

You have angry family syndrome.

Everybody is always on the phone.

The demons continue to drone.

Either the person on the other end rams the phone.

Or the fellow who called up ceases to croak.

They are forever shouting at each other.

They are always at war with others.

They haunt each other's homes.

To spread insecurities,unhappiness and more.

They are truly similar in behaviour.

Though their circumstances are dissimilar.
Sometimes your genes play havoc.
You are victims of your father or grandfather's
Nature.
Either you copy them or it is ingrained in you.
You keep on spoiling your family's routine if not
Their mood.
You should pray to your ancestors not to haunt your
House.
Once they are gone don't let them come back for
More rounds.
It might keep the family happy all the year round.
Don't always nourish your ego so much.
Be understanding towards at least women and
Children.
Whether they are your family members or
Outsiders.
Stay peaceful and calm.
Let your house work like a balm.
Let it not be a place which is haunted.
Untangle anger from your heart.
Overcome your upbringing by default.
Once that happens, life would be happy for all.

137

She was a man eater !

Every boy in her class loved her.

She made a lot of din.

Each one thought she was interested in him.

She was my best friend.

Was I lucky, friends?

Yes,I thought so.

We clicked with each other more and more.

She was so witty I admired her.

I learnt a lot from her.

I frequented her home pretty often.

She even went for a trip with me for fun.

We spent a lot of time with each other.

We went out to have coffee,often with class boys,

Together.

I was though more interested in sharing notes with

Her.

She would almost always outsmart me and others.

I knew why boys always eyed her with interest.

She was a typical saree clad beautiful Indian woman

With one long plait like a snake on her back.

Her communication skills were excellent.

She sure was a charmer always at her best.

Our male classmates were hooked on her.

Each one found her very intelligent.

We had made friends with each other from day
One.

I soon realised, I was often an aid for her plans.

She just wanted to entangle her male fans.

Flirting coquettishly she won over many men.

I often felt she wanted me to come along with her,

So that she could avoid going alone with men,

As I was pretty aloof and seldom thought of boy
Friends,

I never thought of myself as competition.

But a boy from my neighbourhood made friends

With me at the University special bus stand

We chatted with each other now and then.

Sometimes he came to see me in college.

But my best friend got involved with him without
My knowledge.

I felt awkward but couldn't do anything about it.

Anyway I wanted to concentrate on my studies.

But she couldn't lose a potential mate to me.

I felt she had come between me and him.

Nevertheless it pained me when she abruptly
Dumped him.

She just liked flirting with boy friends.

She enjoyed attention from them.

She was no less than a queen in her own eyes.

She made a boy friend for a while and then said
Good bye.

I was not into impressing boys from college.

As far as possible I avoided them.

I was also dressed in simple outfits.

Never thought of being fashionable or hip.

I was time and again reminded by my parents,

That I was sent to college just to have education.

Boy friends could come later.

I had even told this boy about it.

He didn't,however,want to leave me.

If not me at least he could make friends with my

Friend.

Anyway, we graduated and did post graduation

Too.

She got in as a lecturer soon.

I had to wait to get a lecturer's post.

I found she had begun to show an attitude.

I did feel bad about it but I understood.

By and by we drifted apart.

I still miss her a lot, all said and done, she had won

My heart.

But I have no idea where to find her.

She had gradually disappeared.

Friends are for life.

I hope to see her before I die.

138

Do something.
Don't idle away your time.
Be "A tinker, tailor, soldier,sailor, rich man,poor
Man, beggar man, thief,"
As this popular rhyme preached.
If not, be a thinker, actor, police man,
Multimillionaire, model, manager, company chief.
You can even be a delivery boy, a driver, a shop
Keeper, teacher, banker, doctor, surgeon, preacher.
Never be a thief.,
Sorry I plead guilty.
You can be a sales man, musician, writer
Advertiser. vegetable vendor, beautician, barber,
Physiotherapist, prosthetist, petrol pump handler,
Compounder, Store keeper, purser.
Take tuitions in subjects like English, Math or
Computer or science.
German,Italian, French or Japanese.
It is a criminal waste of time if you just stay at
Home without any work.
House wives can be exempted as they have to bring
Up children.
After children are old enough to be under care of
Somebody else for a shift,or begin to go to school,
They can resume work.

Men have absolutely no excuse to keep wandering
Aimlessly and look foolish.
Able bodied men with normal intelligence must
Work.
Just tap all the sources to find work.
You will continue to find it rewarding though
Sometimes tough.
Hunt the entire world,don't sulk.
Somebody will find you soon enough.
Nobody will ever suffer any taunts.
You will win hearts when your work is launched.
Don't lose your confidence.
Everybody has some talent.
Find out your tilt,
Your future will be built.
You will not ever be an outcast,
You will hold your head high and have a blast.

139

I get goose bumps,
And I feel stumped,
When I watch The Republic Day Parade at Raj Path.
My eyes get welled up with tears to see,
The discipline, Unity and Our Cultural Diversity.
From the march past by the Military,
Police, Para Military, NCC and school kids.
The entire spectacle fills us with pride.
Our Mother Land is so versatile.
Since our country became a Republic.
The Republic Day Parade showcases the progress of
The country.
We don't cease to be thankful to our men in the
Forces,
Who stand at borders to protect our country from
The enemy.
We owe our lives to these brave soldiers,
Who sacrifice their life, leaving behind the family in
Tears while guarding our borders.
If we minutely observe our states not just during
Elections but while celebrating their cultural
Heritage,
We can't take our eyes off their folk dances and
Architecture.
Our country 's wide and broad area has rich soil,

Which grows plenty of cereals, vegetables,fruit and
Rice.
Our democracy is a great example of robust system
Of governance.
The secular approach to people welcomes people of
All religions.
I can't praise my country enough.
It has given me everything I could have wished for
As a citizen.
Long live my great country and its humble but
Multitalented people.
I bow to thee my Mother Land,
I am proud to be a citizen of this land.
I salute thee my Nation.
I sure am proud to be its citizen.

140

Hate is toxic
No doubt about it.
It destroys your peace,
It disturbs your routine.
It opens door to demonic,
Beings.
It shakes your confidence
Your hate filled heart
Doesn't fit the bill.
Try not to hate the person
Who is mentally weak,
Who has no control over himself,
Who might even be a beast,
Who had almost been loveless all his life,
Who was a witness to his mother's plight.
She used to be degraded, abused, hit and riled.
Hate his vices.
He has had no role model in his life.
He can be humorous, sincere and good.
But he can't rewrite his childhood.
He cannot erase his genes.
Continue to love him,
Try to survive being hurt by his rough edges.
Teach him what is right.
Teach him to live life.
Teach him to smile.
Sit down, chat with each other for a while.
Stay happy all your life.

141

Follow your dreams.

Those who do, succeed.

Spread your wings and fly.

Even if your destination is not in sight.

Your imagination takes you to great heights.

Sky laden with dark clouds may deter you.

Stop, wait but continue to fly.

You may fly past miles of mountains and cities,

You may land on islands wild and uninhabited,

Silence of the peaks and noise of the streets,

May teach you quite a few lessons in life.

You may sit and mull over what you like.

To think, to question, to comprehend, to realise,

To believe in your self, to strengthen your mind,

Rest your wings, recharge your resolve to rise.

Carry on, your heart and mind must be aligned,

Only then you will achieve your goals in time.

Flying is so exciting and thrilling.

You reach nooks where nobody is visible.

Elegantly drooping deep into undiscovered sites.

Obstacles, pitfalls. speed breakers, spaces wild,

You blink, flutter your wings, perch on a rubble Pile.

Philosophically, take a sigh, awakening to real life.

Begin your journey back to your kith and kin,

Having realised what life is all about all the while.

Inspiration, hope, strong character, determination,
Purpose and definite goals in life suffice.
Never give up, make an effort, keep flying.
Watch and admire who display the art of flying.
Life would certainly be worth while.

142

You are a good host.

You make every guest feel at home.

Still, I hear a woman has no home.

She stays with her father in childhood.

After marriage with her husband.

With her son if she is a widow.

But it is she who makes a house home.

She brings in a feminine touch.

She is good at interior decoration.

She instinctively knows,

How to organize herself and her house.

Besides she is caring and loving

Enough to make the family feel secure.

But,unfortunately, she herself often feels insecure.

The man of the house controls her for sure.

He is quick to blame her,

For any gaffe by any family member.

Including herself.

He is often like a rag picker,

Who keeps picking up faults in every one.

And blames them on her.

With so much negativity in the house,

It falls short of being a home.

Her father,the head of the family,

Took care of her in childhood.

He did not snap at her,
But husbands and sons dictate her,
What to do?
If she loses her husband,
She is at the mercy of her son.
That is if she has aged.
If she is young she goes back to her father,
More often she is married off again.
A woman is treated like property.
She is not considered an independent entity.
She is beguiled as weak.
God has to teach society to give her a home.
A well paid man does make a family house.
He spends all his savings to build this
Accommodation.
But if he and his wife are incompatible,
If they have just made compromises.
They can't build a happy home.
Their children won't have happy memories of
Their home.
It takes a lot of inputs to turn a house,
Into a safe, secure and loving home.
Harmony makes a house comfortable.
Your family feels really at home.
You need to give good values to your children.
Present a model of peace, joy, endurance and love
To them.
Create a heaven of a home secure, a cosy den.

143

Music takes you through riveting streets.

Your feet automatically tap with the beats.

Your neck moves left, right and back again.

You hum along with the voice which is trained.

Your body sways like branches do when it is windy.

You are lost in notes now high now dwindling.

Instrumental music is as enchanting as a flowing
River.

Words sung in tune are as magical as words of a
Lover.

You connect with rhythms expressing pangs of
Longing.

Explicit words often voice your tender feelings.

Shimmering words laden with emotions touch a
Chord.

You are overwhelmed to hear words expressing
Your thoughts.

The colourful notes dance to commands of the tide.

Carry you along,drowning you in tears of joyful
Vibes.

Music is the ultimate aphrodisiac.

Catching you red handed with a desire tag.

Classical music stretches its range of notes to
Heavenly tilts.

You forget all your tensions, your worries bit by bit.

Music diverts your mind leading you to peace and
Quiet.
Channelizing your energies towards better life.
Music is not just some kind of noise,
It is soothing, healing,pleasing, meditating,
Entertaining voice or rhythmic sound.
It keeps you away from brooding.
It makes you healthy and smiling.
A home without music is dull.
Music fills your house with joy and love.
Let there be music in your life.
If you wanna celebrate being alive.

144

Dissent often hurts your sensibilities,
But it denotes freedom of speech.
If you can say what you want to,
It makes you feel wanted.
What you say matters.
If you are snubbed whenever you open your
Mouth,
You feel very upset,no doubt
There is something amiss in this relationship.
There is no equality between the sexes.
They will live a much happier life,
If there is communication between the husband
And wife.
Men in our present day society,
Assume the responsibility of being head of the
Family.
They are Demi Gods for all the kith and kin.
Nobody dare contradict them.
Dissent in public' though can be alarming.
It signifies discontent in the society.
It shouldn't be used for political vendetta.
The authorities must investigate and find out their
Agenda
The guilty shouldn't go unpunished.
If it looks like sedition,

If it seems anti nation.

The government must take a stand.

The dignity of the Nation has to be protected.

If it is by the misguided youth,

They ought to be counselled to remain faithful.

Such dissent just shows rebellion.

It is not a big deal. It can be tackled.

A healthy democracy is good for the country.

Thrashing out the dissent doesn't mash up the

Story.

Agree to disagree is the best policy.

It gives you space to prove your strategy,

Choosing the subject is your prerogative.

Welcome protests if they are genuine.

It shouldn't hurt the sovereignty of your country.

Love your country.

Be caring and loving.

Be hard working,

Earn your living honestly.

Stay healthy and wealthy.

Never betray your country.

145

Most people believe in middle class morality,
They mind their 'p's and 'q's generally.
No excess in drinks, no smoking regularly,
Absolutely no womanizing, no to 'dirty' films.
Whatever is morally wrong or bad for them
Is avoided.
'Follow the middle path" is considered good strategy.
Don't over eat, don't over dress, don't speak much,
Never eat extra spicy food, or never buy too many
Clothes or cosmetics, or splurge on treats to friends.
If they strike a balance in everything they do,
They will be a perfect example of being sensible
People.
But if you are modern, educated,independent
And liberal,
Middle class values are passé.
You take your own stance.
You have the discretion to know what is ok or
What is risqué.
If you still follow the values your parents gave you.
It still makes sense to know what's your take on,
Decisive curves your life takes.
Debating the issues helps.
However, destiny still plays its role.
You may surmise what happens next but you can't
Predict the future on the whole.

Progressive minds often anticipate the outcome,
As they have a scientific temperaments.
Those who research on different topics,
Heavily rely on possibilities and results.
Most working people have the hang of choosing
The right options.
So paltry few are left who advocate middle class
Morality.
That is of course a good sign that society is
Changing.
The young handle their personal lives intelligently.
What was traditionally immoral in some ways is
Moral.
Live in relationships are not frowned upon.
The young men or women do drink.
They are sexually liberated.
The world is changing.
There is no dearth of ideas.
Educated people carve a niche for themselves.
They are constantly at it.
Their ways to create jobs, wealth or comforts,
Single them out.
The world is cleaner, beautiful, and more
Comfortable by and by.
Cities are smart.
The growth in rural areas is fast.
Thumps up for new thoughts and new ideas.
Middle class with narrow mindedness is being
Upgraded at last.

146

Make me a whole soul again, God!

It feels broken at times.

It hurts quite a few times.

It often feels frustrated.

It goes solo at times.

Why should a soul go in depression?

Souls should be above such problems.

I guess, the body and the soul are intertwined.

Bodily hurts shouldn't touch it all the time.

'I am' and 'me' are different.

When they align with each other,

You feel better.

If they are separate from each other,

Why do they die together?

Why are they born together?

There is a mystery there.

Can a doctor create a soul?

Animal clones have been made.

Test tube babies are made.

Animals may not have souls.

TTB have both male and female chromosomes.

So a baby is made but still in the womb.

But a soul per se doesn't exist.

If it does, it is invisible,

Science has yet to discover soul particles.

Whatever,a layman knows your mouth doesn't
Speak by itself.
The systems in the body manage the body.
Though we attribute thoughts and emotions,
To something called the soul.
We go through tough times, good times.
We form impressions, opinions,
We feel pain, bliss, anger, love, hatred.
Our body when hurt,hurts our soul too.
It hurts when our soul is hurt too.
We find it tough to separate them.
They are like two friends who stick to each other.
God I pray that both my body and soul,
Stay calm and collected,
Maintain an equilibrium,
So that I stay both mentally and physically,
Healthy and happy.
That covers all my demands!
Not too difficult to grant me what I want?

147

Hello baby,why are you so glum?
Why must you hide in a corner and sulk?
Go out with a friend or mix around.
It helps you to come round.
Think and count.
There are so many things you like in twos.
Think of things, food and people.
Toothbrush and tooth paste.
Chain and pendant.
Mirror and comb.
Dustpan and broom.
T.V and remote.
Socks and shoe.
Sheet and pillow.
Bulb and lampshade.
Key and key chain.
Lock and key.
Pen and ink.
Needles and wool
Saw and wood.
As for food,
Kidney beans with rice,
Curry with spices.
Bread and butter.
Sushi and horse radish

Chicken and Biryani.

Well! well!

You have enough choices.

Does it help to connect with something?

Yes? No?

Lets get people together.

Nurse and doctor,

Aunt and uncle.

Man and woman,

Teacher and student

King and queen.

Pairs are often an inspiration.

Couples are a joy to see.

Two is company.

You cannot doubt.

The young mix around.

The more the better.

The more the merrier.

They all have fun when together.

Go indulge!

Go have fun!

Go get an ice cream bar.

Share a bite with some one near or far.

Have a blast!

How nice to see you laugh at last!

148

Touch screen has changed the modalities.

You index finger moves with speed and agility.

Opening up a world of unimagined facilities.

Your fingers usually play the sitar, Piano or drums.

They are multi pronged weapons, multi- tasking for Us.

They are used for licking tasty sauces from tins.

They make mixing ingredients easy for cooking.

They help hit a power packed slap when you are Angry.

They help pat somebody's back when needed.

They outshine the face with several crafted rings.

Drive, cook or clean,write or get engaged in Painting,

Your fingers help the hand with a million things.

But the greatest help they do is touch the mobile Screen.

A Magical Box opens up with icons to work with.

They touch the right keys to write fast for us.

Technology has truly won over most of us.

We feel empowered by using our fingers.

Our mobile in our hands explores the universe.

We are awed by the knowledge we get in minutes.

I must fold my hands to thank the inventors.

They have given us a tool to play with almost

Anything!

'Touch' had quirky connotations earlier.

The touch screen mobiles have made us techno

Savvy.

Long live my smartphone and 'Tablet'.

The screens on them have changed my rationale.

149

Your equation with friends varies.

You just connect as colleagues,

You may enjoy partying with some,

You may begin to like someone.

Stay friendly with him for a while.

As you are young and volatile,

You may shift your loyalty to someone else.

You trust him and wanna plan your future

With him.

Unfortunately he falls prey to his family's whims.

You are doing well in your career.

You divert your mind to work.

You have episodes of epiphany,

You discover your life has other meanings.

It is natural to out grow an episode of unrequited

Love.

Love cannot be easily side-tracked though.

Like a warrior you fight your own inner battles.

Overcome palpable passions,

Ignore your heart beats and tension.

Even if you are on a roll in your work field.

In some nook in your heart love lurks painfully.

Resilient that you are,

You have moved on and filled your time with new

activities.

Life runs like a river flowing, taking and making
Automatic turnings.
There are surprises on the way to add thrill to your
Journey.
You finally do settle down with somebody chosen
By destiny.
Of course choices narrow down as you grow older.
Your shelf life as a matrimonial catch is limited.
That's the reason parents push you to marry when
Young.
After a certain age you are on your own.
Parents become too old to interfere in your life.
If you click with a potential match, you marry.
Otherwise you stay single, fulfil your life's mission.
Happy or unhappy, God decides how you live your life's
Vision.
Dreams do not always translate into real
Life.
Somewhere you have to compromise.

150

An eloquent speech does draw you in.
The message it carries,
The passion it carries,
Pulls you along,
You can't help being impressed.
It makes a u turn in your beliefs.
You may even change your sides.
It is not just the content, the arguments
Put forward that pulls you toward it.
It is the way it is presented, the choice of words,
The impact intended, the volume of voice, the
Accent, all count.
Speech must contain facts and purpose.
Silence,they say, speaks volumes.
But only in specific situations.
Generally it is speech which is needed
To express your side of the case.
Silence is used for effect at certain points
In the speech.
The pauses for effect add style to your speech.
Recently a lady minister in the ruling party,
Impressed the members with the delivery of her
Speech.
The way she conveyed her point of view on the
Current hot topics in the Country was impressive.

It engaged even the opposition's attention.
They have been restless,disturbing the
Parliament's proceedings lately.
It was a compliment to the young lady,
To see them being entranced by her performance.
We must salute her for being both bold and
Beautiful. gutsy,honest and efficient.
Such women set an example for the young
Generation.
If women can stand for the Nation,
They can stand for themselves too if the need
Arises.
Women should come forward to discuss what
Matters
Why should they be projected as weak and
Helpless?
Criminal men must be given adequate punishment.
They are a scourge to society.
Women,be strong.
That will be your greatest asset and ammo.

151

Love is not, getting married to you.

It could be a match of convenience.

You are good looking enough and rich.

You come from an educated family.

His parents have chosen you for him.

Fine.

But where does love fit in?

It has yet to be tracked.

You may or may not fall in love.

Sex might kindle love.

It could be something hateful too.

Anyway, there is some stability in your life.

Love is not managing your bank account.

Love is not buying ration for the family.

Love is not, later in life when you are old and weak,

You are taken to hospital if sick.

It is some kind of connection between the couple,

As there is no other go.

It is caring at the most.

Does love mean caring only?

There is some understanding on some level.

Love is not leaving you to look after his family,

While he is away for years working for money.

Love is not putting you down at the drop of a hat.

Reprimanding you for slightest over sight,

Hurting you because he is angry at somebody or
Something else
You are not his punching bag.
Where is love?
By the majority opinion,
You are married,
Isn't that enough?
How you handle it,
Also makes a difference.
The onus is on you to change,
Man the original savage,
To teach him a few tricks,
To win you over!
Forget love.
It is just a concept !
You need only common sense,
To reach the last stretch!

· 152 ·

A woman is not a robotic doll.
She cannot always be at your call.
Molded,twisted any which way you wish.
She may be assertive, certainly not a shrew
she cannot approve everything about you.
She has a right to demand attention from you,
She wants to be loved,
She wishes to be treasured.
She wishes life to be an adventure.
She thinks romance can be created.
Just eating, sleeping, working,
Watching TV or listening to music,
Is not exactly romance.
A man must learn how to treat his counter part.
How to soften his speech, choose words,
Carefully,learn to win her heart.
Try asking her what she likes and why,
What she would like to buy for them and home
Decore.
Where she would like to go,
Why not plan to go together for a vacation abroad.
She may want a new wardrobe,
She may want you to wear your choicest robes.
Actually it is not so difficult to please your wife.

Small little gestures win her heart with time.
Try it if you want both of you to celebrate your life.
Your memories together will be incentive enough,
To live a long life with love.

153

Fix the world.

Fine tune it.

But how?

You can't change it all.

Stay on the right side of the law.

If crime was annihilated,

What a weight would be moved away from the
World.

If wars are not needed to maintain peace,

If nuclear bombs stop being built in any country,

Security will be boosted in everybody's mind.

If the sea, the rivers, the lakes and the ponds,

Stay full with clean water that shines,

If love is not betrayed world wide,

If twinkling stars and the moon peep at you from
The sky,

If children bloom like colourful flowers,

Each finds space to play and have a blast,

If grand parents sit on the benches in the parks,

And feel overwhelmed to see their grand sons and,

Daughters playing energetically with all,

If grown ups handle their problems fast,

If infrastructure every where is world class,

If the last terrorist is transformed into a law abiding,

Citizen,

If con men stop cheating innocent people,
If smiles on every face are visible,
If Bollywood or Hollywood continue to churn out,
Meaningful films,
If no visas are needed to cross over to
Neighbouring countries.
If it is not a crime to enter just about any country.
If the governments are people friendly,
If corruption is eliminated from the face of the
Earth.
If every person knows his worth,
If education is free for all,
If every one gets a suitable job,
Have I fixed it all?
The crux of the matter is,
The world should be a happy and progressive place
To live in.
I hope better sense prevails all over the world.
Our dream comes true for a better world.

154

Moment to moment,
Life inches towards its end.
What you remember,
What you forget,
Matters at best.
Love pushes the cart all along.
Hate speeches, hate actions,
Hate crimes, perverted minds,
Egos scaling high,
Verbal slinging matches
Rolling pins and chopping boards,
Going haywire, making folks duck,
To avoid being hit and irretrievably hurt.
To cap it all,divorce rate goes up and up,
Leaving the children bewildered and troubled.
Where is the world going?
Where do we find peace?
Politics around frustrates you.
Terrorism kills innocent troupes.
Why can't they stop this mayhem?
The circle we live in becomes narrower.
Weaving a tangled skein of wool,
Escape from the wickedness of the fools,
Escape from the personal stuffy spaces,
Becomes impossible and tacky.

Moment to moment life slows down.

You wanna live but go round and round.

Life must regain its crown.

Never give up,let your health stay sound.

It is your might and high morale that will win you,

Several rounds.

155

A woman doesn't believe in words.

She wants raw passion.

She will go to any length to please her man.

But she doesn't like being ignored for any reason.

She becomes belligerent if snubbed,

She hits you hard with killing expressions.

She can even secretly follow you all around the
Town.

Turn your cupboard upside down

She has the knack of pinning you down.

She wanna live like a queen and wear the crown.

A woman has powers a wrestler won't have.

She becomes an omnipotent, omniscient presence.,

If challenged.

She is so possessive and adamant,

She won't allow any woman to look at her man.

God save you,man, from atrocities of women

A man is so carefree.

He thinks women are just to be seen.

He just puts his head in the news paper,

Pretending to be involved in something serious.

If his woman is around trying to catch his attention.

He sleeps like a log on a holiday from work.

Like a well heeled woman she terms him a jerk.

Meals have to be elaborate on such days,

She resents being treated like a maid.
Man knows how to handle such petty problems.
His cool ways stump every one.
He will take the whole family out to have dinner.
Thus end up being a pampering husband. and
Father.
He goes about his rendezvous without any guilt.
Leads a hip and trendy life style nonchalantly.
Marriage is just a ruse to sort of settle down.
It is not something you do to red paint the town.
Marriage doesn't exactly tie you down,
It gives you a licence to freely go around the town.
You can have a stag party to let your hair down.
Work happily and never have a reason to frown.
Let your house run well without any financial
Worries,
You will lead a reasonably happy life daily.

156

When love bug bites you,
You become blind and mute.
The object of your love looks extraordinary.
Your behaviour towards him is over sweet.
Both put on their best foot forward.
They do whatever it takes to woo each other.
They neglect their duties towards their family.
They are generally generous with everybody.
Usually the man keeps his head in the right place.
But God save the woman!
She throws common-sense to the winds.
Lovingly empties her hard earned money on him!
She becomes more daring in her speech and action.
Man on the other hand is just interested in messing
Around with her.
He suddenly begins to throw invitations to her.
Once they get a chance to be close to each other,
They begin to behave normal.
They cool down to an extent.
At this stage awareness begins to dawn on them,
They are part of the bigger picture of family and
Friends.
They just can't afford to play around with ease.
Life is not exactly open to love birds' cosy scenes.
Meeting on the sly, they begin to feel guilty.
Either they decide to end the escapade quickly,

Or if they really are into serious relationship,
And see a future of this alliance surely,
They carry on the affair nonchalantly.
Western world calls it dating.
Sometimes even infidelity!
We call it pure infatuation.
A temporary attraction.
It will die down with time.
They will realise all is not exactly fine.
Either they gradually call it quits,
Or announce it bit by hit.
It might shock the family.
They might have to put a break to their meetings.
If sense prevails they will discreetly put an end to it.
Or carry on boldly.
Chances are they will not extend the story.
Part for good as the affair was just not flourishing.
Two souls,to sum up, inadvertently ran into each
Other in this life.
Reminded them selves perhaps they had met in
Previous Lives.
But real life now has different challenges,
They cannot just connect to events in past life foolishly.

They must be grateful to the almighty,
They spent lovely moments together even though Briefly.
Their memories should suffice,
To carry on their duties in this life.

157

Digging into a book is the best exercise,
In terms of mental health.
Sudoku, Chess or Scrabble too help.
Not only do they keep you busy,
Alzheimers too is kept at bay.
If reading paper books puts a strain on your eyes,
Try listening to audio books some times.
Font on e-books can be enlarged for you.
It is less straining than reading a bound book.
Games apps are easy to download,
There is no problem on that score.
Why then can't we do a favour to ourselves?
Keep doing mental acrobatics to save ourselves.
Physical exercise is sure mandatory to stay fit.
Equally important is the stuff you eat.
Just don't take chances with your health issues.
They keep bouncing back to trouble you.
If you have a job or business,fine.
Your fiscal health too decides your track in life.
Your education prepares you to follow a career.
You have to manage both home and work,
Without compromising on your fundamentals.
Keep your fun quotient live.
Stay healthy,stay disease free and fine.
Loving yourself as much as you love others,

You can withstand all the shocks that life showers.
It would be a good idea to learn to play an
Instrument.
Music keeps you in a meditation mode,
Your quality of life gets the highest score.
Getting involved in political debates,
Tension begins to reign.
It rusts your brain.
You begin to feel brickbats rain.
Reading fiction,biographies and what have you,
Changes your life style and brings you under
Who is Who.
Shun the newspapers, shun news channels if you
Want to stay sane.
Think about these game changers again and again.
Become members of some good libraries in your
City,
Borrow classics, latest best sellers,even music CDs,
Watch Oscar winning films
Or entertaining Bollywood films.
Your favourite hero and heroines,
Attend cultural programmes in the evenings.
Follow a rich,content, inspiring and fulfilled routine.

158

Hickory Dickory Dock,

Life doesn't always rock.

Yack yak yakety yack

You try to be on the right track

You get derailed once in a while.

Drift along with winds wild.

Familiar fields turn hostile.

You have to follow your destiny.

Play whatever cards you are dealt with.

You may own Aces,Kings and Queens,

The game often becomes interesting.

Win or lose, lose or win

life is constantly throwing challenges.

You learn to duck when hit.

Hug those who help you win.

Growing up is done in stages.

You have guidance in your tough phases.

Rivers have one way flow,

Following them is not a load.

But twists and turns tax your strength.

Your motivation takes you ahead then.

Walk, jog or run.

Life is not always fun.

A lot depends on how you handle it.

Get a breather if you think fit.

But get up and get going,
that Is the only way to surviving.
Winning is not the goal per se.
Kick in your butt,
Get grounding in some work.
Have enough moolah to live it up.
Stay connected with family and friends.
After all they add that zing to your existence.

159

Breaking news, breaking news.

A doctor is on the loose,

Beware of him,

His job is to hook patients,

For Cat Scans, Ultra Sound and MRIs.

The bait is placebo for any disease.

He draws a crowd around him,

His smile is worth seen.

He doesn't become a millionaire for nothing.

Breaking news,breaking news.

Leaders of opposition united today,

To back up each other for disrupting the debate.

What fun to get their inflated salaries for nothing.

Public money goes for a spin.

Country takes the back burner.

Cast politics takes the stage at centre.

Breaking news,breaking news

Bollywood is seeking Hollywood,

Top heroines are seen on the red carpet,

Local ones are cash strapped,

Catch the local from home to studio and back.

Films based on real life are the craze,

Old classics remakes are back in race.

Breaking news, breaking news.

A wife fakes an abduction by kidnappers,

Just to remind her husband she is not an induction
Cooker,
If he doesn't learn to take care of her,
She might take a more drastic action.
Her fake kidnapping has a shocking value.
Her family,her husband must be tense and blue.
Breaking news, breaking news.
Roads have been made so wide and concrete,
They are good enough for foot ball fields.
No traffic is seen for hours,
No pollution so far.
The world seems to be upside down.
What's right or what's wrong?
Breaking news always threatens to be disturbing.
It is actually ridiculous and freaking funny.
TV has a million fascinating tourist friendly sites
And cuisines to show.
Watch them to learn the world cultures instead of
Bleak political,ridiculous, newsy shows.
Breaking news has broken my back.
Will somebody fix it or I go to a quack?

160

No doubt your decisions and innovations
Pave a way for the next generation.
You try to leave a better world for your children.
Every generation is more evolved and presentable.
Evolution does take place refining man's existence.
Unfortunately ugliness in the society is hidden from
View,
The way young ones are misled is preposterous but
True.
Crimes against women and juveniles are
Multiplying.
We shudder to think of the consequences on them
And their families.
We are warned about alerts in TV serials.
You shudder in your boots to realise they are not
Surreal.
Positive,selfless,efficient, wise and bold leaders
Are few and far between,
Our illiterate or semi literate citizens just tow the
Line.
Awareness of their rights and duties is the last
Thing on their minds.
Basic education,health insurance with treatment at
State of the art hospitals is every citizen's right.
If population goes on increasing, everything would

Go on being divided.

Progress will be hampered,

Educating the masses is a humongous responsibility,

The government has to have patience to implement

Progressive schemes.

Fortunately we are a rich nation with vital

Resources.

We must resolutely follow our social

Responsibilities.

Enrich the society with better outcomes of our

Policies.

Irresponsible political opponents mustn't be

Allowed to, thwart democratic functioning of the

Parliament.

The government must keep the onus of progress on

Their heads.

March with the team,our reverent head,

Hold your head high to run the government,

Punctuating victories every where in our land.

We will sing along with you,

Celebrating every moment of success with you,

Long live our mother land,we are proud of you.

161

When you review the previous day,
You feel you have valiantly survived another day.
Nothing much happens these days.
There is no goal to chase.
Just survival is your aim.
All the systems in your body work,
Every organ reasonably functions.
Your mind no longer wanders into any nook and
Cranny.
The quiet that resides within is zany.
Your aches and pains stay with you.
They accompany you as an integral part of you.
Balms of all kinds,a few doses of medicines,
Keep oiling the brittle bones and weak muscles.
Nature heals if your body moves,
Prayer on your lips helps you improve.
You now book only a day's package with God,
Renew it every day as you feel better a lot.
Some redeeming features also exist,
To bring back some fun activities.
Looking back to youthful days,
There was hardly time to indulge in regrets.
You just continued to do your best at work,
Mingled around with family members and
Neighbours.
Travelling to and fro from work consumed,

A big chunk of your time,
You were always too tired and sleepy to enjoy,
Your free time.
Life jumped over many years at a go.
That you were older never registered,though.
Going through your track then, you notice grey hair,
Middle age spread and slower gait.
Change comes so stealthily,you don't even notice.
If you run into an old acquaintance,
And she feels you have lost or gained weight,
You know you have moved to an older stage.
Before you know, you are a revered grand parent,
Children flock around you to vie for sitting on your
Lap.
If you think you are still young enough to follow
Fashion,
Try to get into Facebook, twitter or what's App.
You do handle online shopping with élan.
If you refuse to acknowledge your age,
Keep up with the smartphone technology,
You win the envious slot of being techno savvy and
Happening.
You wow your colleagues who can't handle,
Tablets, smartphones and IPads,
You chill with young ones as you click with all of
Them.
As they say,"Age is just a number"
It is all in the mind.
You are as young as ever.

162

International Women's Day was here once again.
My blood boiled but in vain.
Tall claims were made to raise the status of women.
Ground reality put a different robe on them.
It is frustrating to read the morning news paper.
You shudder to read about gang rapes of young
Women.
How stalkers shoot at or kidnap young females.
How newly married girls are duped by NRI,
Husbands.
How wives have to put up with domestic violence,
How women are victims of dowry deaths,
How they become the butt of ridicule because of
Their surname.
How they are butchered by parents or brothers
Under the guise of honour killing,
Just because they happen to fall in love with
Somebody from another community.
How callous of the world to celebrate one measly
Day as International women's day,
I wish women are thought of everyday,
I wish they are not treated like sexual toys,
I wish their moral strenght,their capacity to,
Sail through tough times,
Their ability to smile,

And so many unique qualities special to them,
Were taken note of by men.
A woman is the loveliest creature on Earth.
It is my prayer to the men's world,
Please honour the women at home and outside.
I bet they will return this favour in manifold styles

163

I am a free spirit today.

I may have been a failure in life in some way.

But today I stand in front of the world,

Displaying the mechanics of my words.

I take pride in my attitude and stride

I stand alone doing exactly what I like.

My mind stands tall celebrating my life.

I want to yell to announce my freedom,

From fiefdom.

How wonderful to flow with your body,

Rejoice in whatever is reverent and holy.

The movements of my body show my energy,

My heart flies up in the sky touching the infinity.

My soul brightens up,perks up and radiates happily.

O almighty,the world may not have changed at all,

But I have evolved into a liberated being who now

Stands tall.

There has to be a time in a woman's life when she

Wakes up to realise her worth.

It had better be now than later.

Dear women,listen to the wake up call.

Discover your power.

Use it to march forward and improve your lot.

You are wished well by all.

164

Explore your mind,

A lot of treasure you will find.

You don't need a spiritual guru to do that.

Just go within yourself,meditate and remember God.

The essence of life will emerge from behind the clouds.

The blue sky will be visible waiting to be found.

The birds will fly past you fluttering to salute you.

The beasts on earth will be peaceful around you.

The treasure you are looking for lies within you.

Don't run helter skelter seeking the real you.

You are a divine being,

Sent on this Earth to seek.

Find links with similar souls,

They often stray into different roads.

Together you can achieve enlightenment.

Be part of the bigger picture at the end.

Glob trotting satiates your curiosity.

Whets your hunger for knowledge.

It is what you have been craving for ages.

Once you put your feet on this endearing planet,

You do not wish to leave this place.

Let your body and soul fight together,

They will conquer all the diminishing returns.

Without efforts nothing is gained wherever you

Stay,

Keep paddling your boat to the other end.

Who knows you will achieve your ends.

Life is all about living it up.

You mustn't chuck anything up.

Every experience makes you wiser in some way.

So you are a satori all the way!

This is the epiphany of your tale.

165

When you leave this world,
You do not own anything material.
Your memory bank also leaves you then.
Why not disperse your wealth and assets,
Collect only the essentials to survive.
Declutter your house and your mind.
Give away heavy furniture, decore and goods in
Your boxes and jewellery lockers,
Donate surplus money to the needy.
Your albums with family pictures can be passed on,
To those who figure in the pictures.
Become a minimalist in terms of owning things.
Worrying about anything shortens you life.
Let your mind stay peaceful and right.
Functional style will shift the load of worldly riches,
To the next generation.
Imagine you do not need to stack up clothes in your
Cupboard.
You don't need to check up your bank lockers,
You do not have to think about matching accessories.,
Or spend a fortune on travelling by air to exotic,
Places.
Do walk down to the nearby places,
Enjoy surrounding nature's beauty.
Do not talk about what you didn't get in life.

Think of all the pleasant people who touched your life.
Think of the good times you had with friends and family.
Why not get into some social causes.
You have lived enough for your kin and yourself.
Concentrate now on life within.
Stay peaceful, gentle and sweet.
You don't need to tweet,go to FB or Instagram,
To declare your Will.
When you cease to be,
Thanks to the digital world.
Everybody will receive the news instantly.
You have yet to taste the bliss of being a spirit.
You are still a worldly being.
Think positive but think like a minimalist.
Survive this ascetic avatar and be simplistic.